BRAZIL

BRAZIL

By the Editors of Time-Life Books

TIME-LIFE BOOKS · AMSTERDAM

A CHILD'S FIRST LIBRARY OF LEARNING
VOYAGE THROUGH THE UNIVERSE
MYSTERIES OF THE UNKNOWN
TIME-LIFE HISTORY OF THE WORLD
FITNESS, HEALTH & NUTRITION
HEALTHY HOME COOKING
UNDERSTANDING COMPUTERS
THE ENCHANTED WORLD
LIBRARY OF NATIONS
HOME REPAIR AND IMPROVEMENT
CLASSICS OF EXPLORATION
PLANET EARTH
PEOPLES OF THE WILD
THE EPIC OF FLIGHT
THE SEAFARERS
WORLD WAR II
THE GOOD COOK
THE TIME-LIFE ENCYCLOPAEDIA
OF GARDENING
THE GREAT CITIES
THE OLD WEST
THE WORLD'S WILD PLACES
LIFE LIBRARY OF PHOTOGRAPHY
TIME-LIFE LIBRARY OF ART
GREAT AGES OF MAN
LIFE SCIENCE LIBRARY
LIFE NATURE LIBRARY

TIME
LIFE
BOOKS

TIME-LIFE BOOKS

EUROPEAN EDITOR: Ellen Phillips
Design Director: Ed Skyner
Director of Editorial Resources: Gillian Moore
Chief Sub-Editor: Ilse Gray
Assistant Design Director: Mary Staples

LIBRARY OF NATIONS

Series Editor: Ellen Galford

Editorial Staff for *Brazil*
Editor: Martin Leighton
Researcher: Lesley Coleman
Designer: Lynne Brown
Sub-Editor: Frances Dixon
Picture Department: Pamela Marke, Christine Hinze,
   Peggy Tout
Editorial Assistant: Molly Oates

EDITORIAL PRODUCTION
Production Assistants: Nikki Allen, Maureen Kelly
Editorial Department: Theresa John, Debra Lelliott

CONSULTANTS: Robert Harvey is a regular contributor to *The Economist*, London, and a member of the British House of Commons; Isabel Hilton is Latin-American correspondent of *The Sunday Times*, London.

Contributors: The chapter texts were written by Douglas Botting, Richard Bourne, Sue Branford, Frederic V. Grunfeld and Patrick Knight.

Cover: Silhouetted against a threatening sky, a 38-metre statue of Christ the Redeemer dominates the city of Rio de Janeiro from the 704-metre summit of the Corcovado (Hunchback) Mountain.

Pages 1 and 2: The emblem on page 1, which includes the date on which the Brazilian Empire became a republic, is surrounded by branches of coffee and tobacco plants. The green background of the national flag on page 2 symbolizes the agricultural wealth of the country, and the golden diamond shape its huge mineral resources. In the centre of the flag, the motto "Order and Progress" is set against a map of the constellations as they appear over Rio de Janeiro.

Front and back endpapers: A topographical map showing the major rivers, mountain ranges and other natural features of Brazil appears on the front endpaper; the back endpaper shows the country's 26 states and territories, and the principal towns.

This volume is one in a series of books describing countries of the world—their natural resources, peoples, histories, economies and governments.

ISBN 0 7054 0855 8

TIME-LIFE is a trademark of Time Warner Inc. U.S.A.

D.L.TO:1013-1990

▲XXX

CONTENTS

1

17
South America's Striving Giant
34 Picture Essay: The Beach as a Way of Life

2

43
Quests and Conquests

3

63
Rich and Poor, Black and White
78 Picture Essay: Cowboys of the Pampas

4

87
An Economic Roller Coaster
105 Picture Essay: Building Itaípu: A Colossus Among Dams

5

113
A Cultural Melting Pot
129 Picture Essay: Land of Many Gods

6

137
Opening Up the Last Frontier

156 Acknowledgements
156 Picture Credits
156 Bibliography
158 Index

Nestling between the mountains and the sea, Rio de Janeiro justifies its reputation as one of the most beautiful cities in the world. The white sweep of the famed Copacabana Beach *(centre)*, fringed by hotels and apartment buildings, connects with downtown Rio *(right)* through a series of tunnels.

THE VANISHING GUARDIANS OF THE GRASSLANDS

Like the cowboys of the North American West, the *gaúchos* of Brazil used to tend herds of cattle that ranged freely over the pampas of the southern states. Now, although the grasslands are fenced in and jeeps have become a common mode of transport, the *gaúchos* still maintain a proud tradition of horsemanship and cultivate a spirit of self-reliance which is very similar to that of the cowboys of Hollywood mythology.

The *gaúchos* are, however, part of a diminishing breed since Brazil, in a mere 40 years, has switched from being a predominantly agricultural to an industrial society, a turnabout that went hand in hand with the country's rapid urbanization. In 1940, 68 per cent of the economically active population were engaged in agriculture, and only 13 per cent in manufacturing and mining; by 1980, only 30 per cent were in agriculture, while the percentage of those in manufacturing, mining and construction had doubled. In the same period those in services grew from 19 per cent to 46 per cent *(chart, below)*.

In addition to the shift into manufacturing and service industries, the number of agricultural workers is declining due to modernization of farming methods. Many ranchers have introduced foreign strains of cattle and now increasingly feed them scientifically rather than by natural pasturage.

Posed proudly on his horse, a *gaúcho* from Rio Grande do Sul wears the trappings of his calling. His traditional *bombachas*, baggy trousers, are tucked into

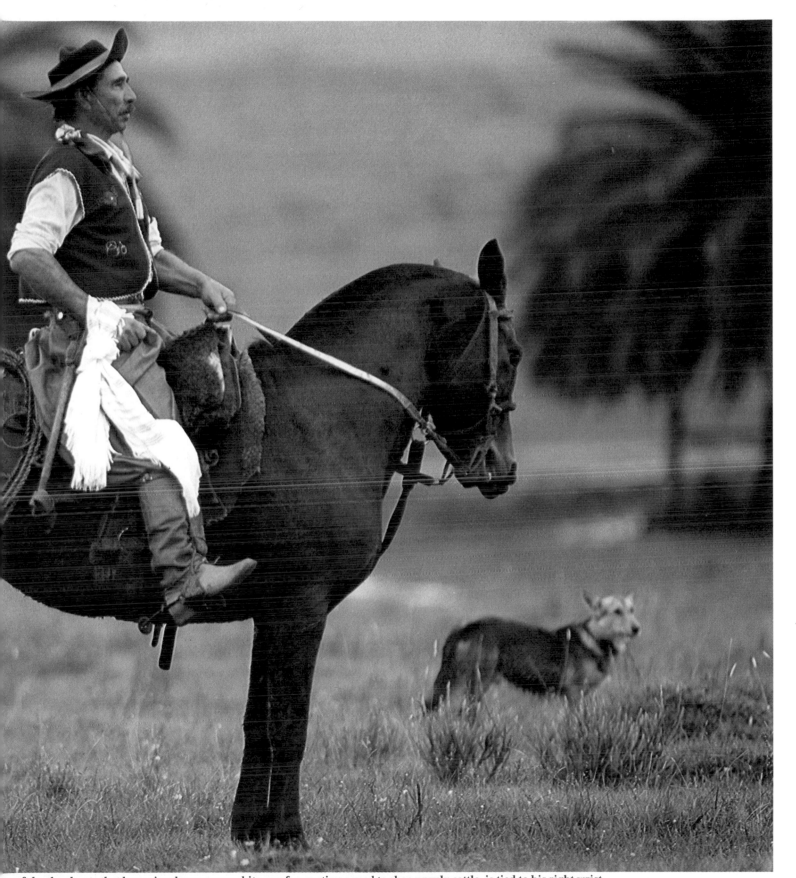

soft leather boots that have circular spurs; a white scarf, sometimes used to shoo unruly cattle, is tied to his right wrist.

RIO'S SAMBA EXTRAVAGANZA

Carnival—for many Catholics, a final fling before Lent—is celebrated throughout Brazil with spectacular parades, music and dancing in which the samba has become an essential element. No Carnival, however, compares with that of Rio de Janeiro, whose untrammelled high spirits and extravagance have made it Brazil's biggest tourist attraction.

Rio's festival culminates in an 80,000-strong parade of Carnival societies, called samba schools, competing for the title of Champion of the Avenue. Some schools spend up to $500,000 a year on the costumes of troupes that can number 3,000 members. To meet the bills, some have turned from amateur societies into big business ventures that put on year-round shows in Brazil and abroad, sell records and publish magazines.

Over a third of the 1.7 million annual visitors to Brazil come for the Rio Carnival. But a growing number of foreign visitors are drawn by no less spectacular natural tourist attractions, such as the Iguaçu Falls in the south, the seemingly endless tropical beaches of Brazil's Atlantic seaboard, and the mysterious Amazon river, best seen from the city of Manaus.

In the nine-hour continuous parade that climaxes Rio's Carnival, a samba school gyrates down the Sambódromo, a 600-metre avenue in the city centre flanked by permanent stands and theatre boxes. The schools are divided into three leagues and are judged on dancing as well as on costumes and floats.

A YOUTHFUL POPULATION

Brazil is not only a young nation in historical terms, but also demographically. With 130 million inhabitants, the country has one of the world's fastest-growing populations: half of it aged less than 20, and 65 per cent under 30. The birth rate, however, is much higher in rural areas, where peasant households average six children compared with three in urban families. A consequence is that the infant mortality rate varies considerably: in the poor, sparsely populated north-eastern states it is as high as 140 per thousand, against 54 per thousand in the urbanized south.

The occupants of a single house in the town of Juàzeiro do Norte, in the north-eastern state of Ceará, gather on their small step. Such extended families are

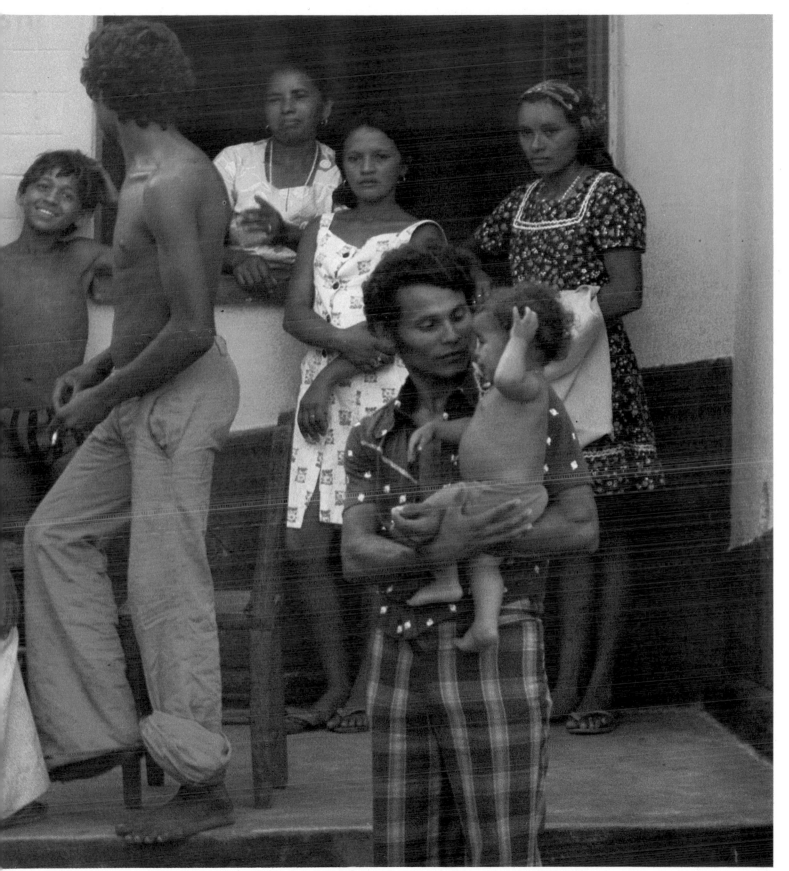

typical in this arid region, where the men earn their livings as subsistence farmers or as peons on sugar plantations.

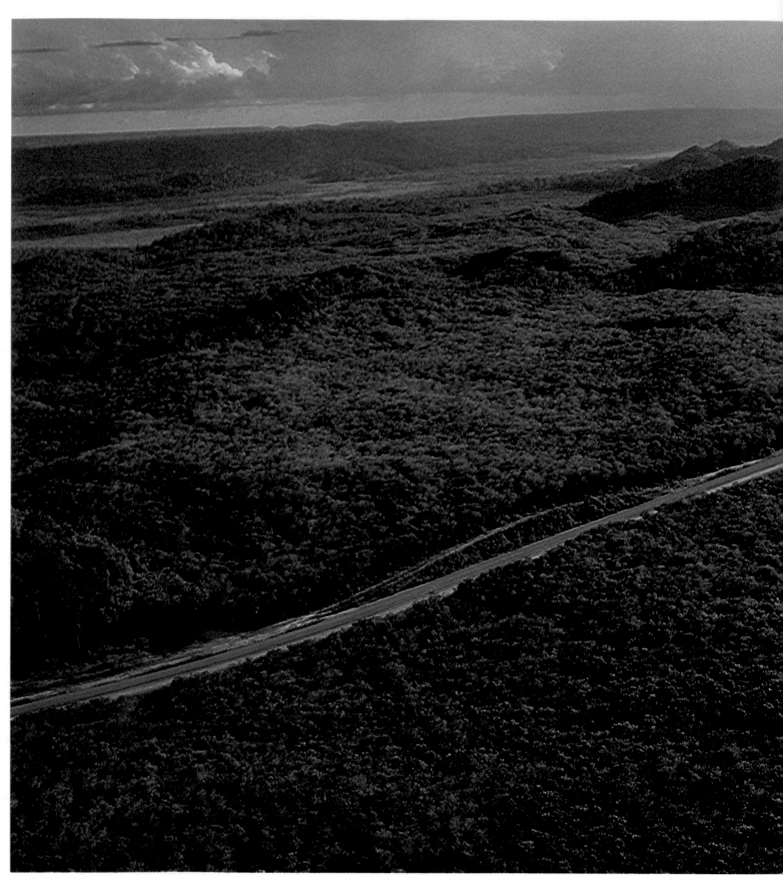

A newly constructed road cuts through primeval rainforest near Jari, north of the Amazon river. Hastily built during the 1970s and for the most part

HIGHWAYS THROUGH A WILDERNESS

Until the late 1950s much of Brazil's vast hinterland remained unexplored and uninhabited except by Indians. But after the establishment of Brasília as the country's new capital in 1960, a massive road-building programme was embarked upon, to open up undeveloped territories.

The first new roads to be built connected Brasília to Belém, in the Amazon estuary, to Pôrto Velho in Rondônia, and to Manaus, capital of Amazonas State. By 1976, there were 2,700 kilometres of paved road and 14,700 kilometres of rough road in Amazonia, including the 4,300-kilometre-long Trans-Amazonian Highway which crosses Brazil from west to east.

The new roads brought an influx of ranchers and peasant settlers to the states of Rondônia, Mato Grosso and Pará. But indiscriminate forest clearance and farming often exhausted the land and so created major ecological problems.

— TRANS-AMAZONIAN HIGHWAY
— NORTHERN PERIMETER HIGHWAY
— PAN-AMERICAN HIGHWAY
— BELÉM-BRASÍLIA HIGHWAY
— OTHER MAJOR ROADS

MACAPÁ · BELÉM · Amazon river · MANAUS · CRUZEIRO DO SUL · PÔRTO VELHO · JOÃO PESSOA · RECIFE · SALVADOR · BRASÍLIA · RIO DE JANEIRO · PÔRTO ALEGRE

unpaved, many highways in Amazonia have proved extremely expensive to maintain and are often impassable during rainy seasons.

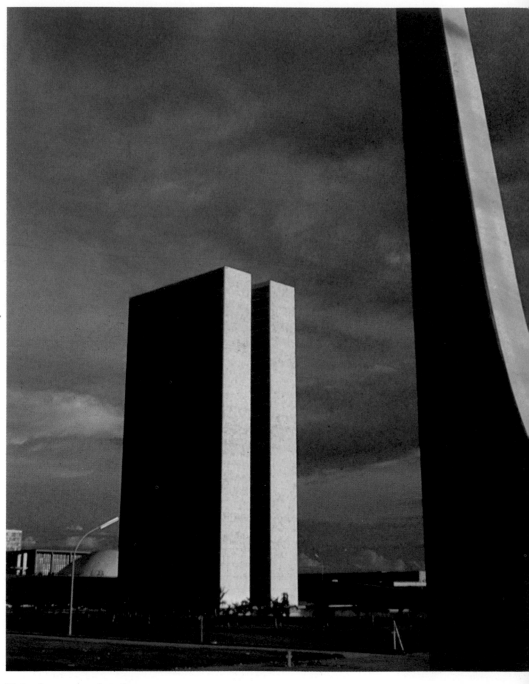

Twin skyscrapers housing parliamentary offices soar above the main square of Brasília, the capital completed in 1960. The young city stands at the centre of a new transportation and communications network which has opened up the vast Brazilian hinterland.

SOUTH AMERICA'S STRIVING GIANT

For more than 150 years, Brazilians talked about building a capital city in the heart of their vast country. The reasons were compelling. Rio de Janeiro, the capital since 1763, was a sea port whose cultural and economic horizons faced over the Atlantic Ocean, to the neglect of its hinterland, a territory 15 times larger than France. Between the late 18th century and the middle of the 20th, various proposals for a new capital were made, but it was not until 1955 that a site was finally selected—nearly 6,000 square kilometres of semi-arid scrubland 1,000 metres up on the Goiás plateau, more than four hours by road from the nearest sizeable town and 1,000 kilometres from Rio de Janeiro.

Even then the project might have foundered but for the dynamism of the republic's newly elected president, Juscelino Kubitschek, who was convinced that the transfer of the capital from the coast was essential if Brazil was to look in upon itself and develop its huge agricultural and mineral resources. In September 1956, Kubitschek signed a state order establishing an umbrella construction body, Novacap (short for New Capital); he thus set in motion the greatest city-building project of the 20th century.

A plan for the new capital, which was to be called Brasília, had been chosen in a competition open to the country's architects. Drawn by Lúcio Costa, the winning proposal set the city along two main axes, crossing at right angles, one of them curved like the wing of an aeroplane. Oscar Niemeyer, the internationally famous architect whose work includes the United Nations building in New York, was commissioned to design the principal buildings. Massive loans were obtained to finance the project: all that was needed were the raw materials and a labour force able to work to a crippling schedule, for Kubitschek had set the inauguration date of the new capital for April 21, 1960.

Novacap recruited its labour force from a massive influx of migrants from the drought-depressed north-east, and to house them it built an encampment 25 kilometres outside the city. Called Free City because it was exempted from taxes, it grew into a wild, sprawling town that looked like a Hollywood set for a Western, with wooden-fronted buildings and false second storeys, unpaved streets and rickety board sidewalks—all coated in the ubiquitous red dust of the region. Jeeps rather than horses were parked in front of the 101 bars, 30 hotels and 35 boarding houses in Free City, and these offered accommodation and entertainment at astronomic prices.

For most of the town's 45,000 inhabitants there was little time to relax. They often worked as many as 15 hours a day, sometimes grabbing a rest while a draughtsman hastily put the finishing touches to a design for a

17

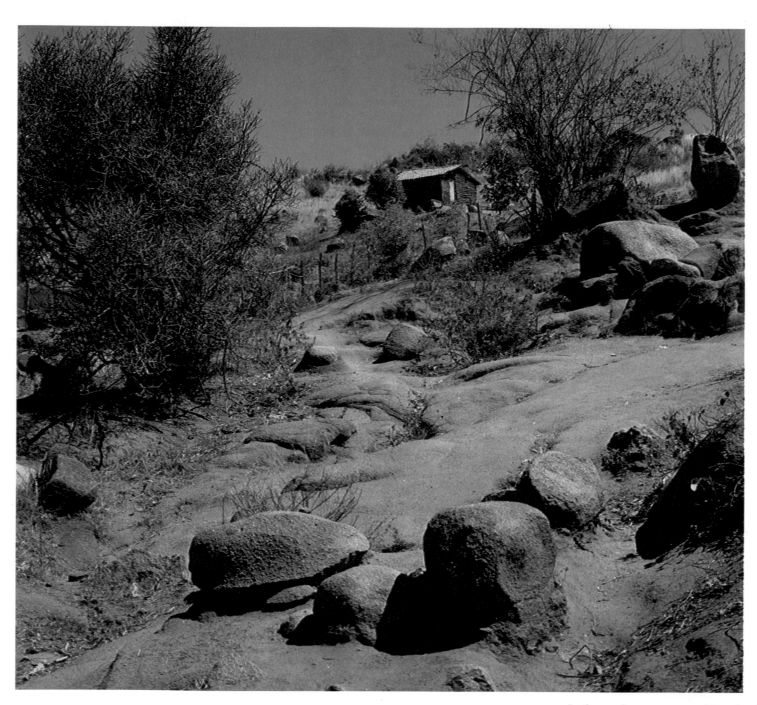

In the north-eastern state of Ceará, where the annual rainfall averages less than 700 millimetres, a landscape of scrub and stone bakes under a cloudless sky. Most of the inhabitants of the area, which is the hottest and driest of Brazil, live at subsistence level, as cattle farmers.

building already under construction. Thanks to these indefatigable *candangos*, as the immigrants from the northeast are called, Kubitschek was able to keep to his planned timetable. On the chosen day, after fewer than five years of construction, the new capital was formally inaugurated. No matter that most of the hotels and apartment buildings were still unfurnished; that the foreign newspaper correspondents slept on straw mattresses on the floors of windowless houses; and that the inaugural mass was held in an unfinished cathedral. Brasília was launched with fanfares and fireworks—not only was it the world's first wholly modern city, but it was also the capital of a far-flung nation that was giving notice to the world that it was taking its place in the 20th century and staking its claim to the 21st.

As might be expected, many Brazilians were opposed to the grandiose scheme. Back in Rio, Senate debates about financial scandals involving Novacap turned into brawls. Any estimate of the cost involved would be a guess, but, by the time the new capital was inaugurated, expenditure on it had exceeded the total amount of currency that had been in existence in Brazil when Kubitschek took office; the country's foreign borrowings had got so out of hand that it was already in trouble with the International Monetary Fund; and domestic inflation had also soared.

Many government employees were unhappy about moving away from Rio; some of them were concerned that their property investments would suffer once the city ceased to be the capital, and all of them were dismayed at the prospect of living in a city so far from the sea, for coastal Brazilians tend to judge a city by the beaches it keeps. Kubitschek enticed the doubters by offering a 100 per cent salary increase to civil servants prepared to work in Brasília. It took longer to persuade foreign embassies to make the move, and for some state corporations to leave the commercial centres of Rio and São Paulo, but by 1974 all government business was being conducted from the new capital.

Today, Brasília has a population of more than a million, living in eight satellite towns. Some of the earliest buildings are cracking, but the capital still looks like a showpiece of the space age—an architectural model of itself—with acres of glass reflecting the futuristic wedges and curves of Niemeyer's buildings, laid out on broad avenues crossed by spectacular underpasses and flyovers.

It is not a pedestrian's city. Only cars move on the streets, giving the city a strangely deserted, even sinister, look—a "terrifying preview of a collectivist future," commented the American historian Arthur Schlesinger. Nor is it a city for the proletariat. Although a grateful government erected

A superimposed map shows that Brazil, stretching over 8,511,965 square kilometres, could easily swallow Europe from the Irish coast to the East German border. However, fewer than 15 people inhabit each square kilometre of the world's fifth largest country, which covers nearly half of South America.

1

a monument in the centre of the city to the *candangos* who had built Brasília, those same workers were relentlessly expelled and set up their own *favelas*, or shanty towns, outside the city limits. Many of these *favelas* stand cheek by jowl with affluent suburbs of red-tiled houses set beside green lawns and blue swimming pools.

Yet even with its *favelas* and glaring inequalities of wealth, Brasília stands as the most spectacular symbol of Brazil's transformation from a quasi-colonial agricultural economy into a modern industrial state. It is a country that has been called a land of never-ending impossibilities—a land which has the eighth largest economy in the Western world and owes more abroad than any other country; a land where an executive can earn 200 times more than a worker, but where the 30,000 richest men pay an average of 1.3 per cent of their incomes in taxes; a land with one of the most rapidly growing populations in the world, but with half its territory no more densely populated than the Sahara Desert. How these contradictions will be resolved is unclear. Brazil is poised, like an imago newly emerged from its chrysalis, drying its wings and still vulnerable, on the threshold of an unpredictable political and economic future.

This transformation is taking place against the backdrop of a truly gigantic physical geography. With an area of 8.5 million square kilometres, Brazil takes up 47 per cent of South America and is the fifth largest country in the world, after the U.S.S.R., Canada, China and the U.S. Moreover, it has more potentially useful territory than any other country in the world, since it has neither inaccessible mountains, burning deserts nor frozen wastes. About three eighths of this territory

20

lies in the basin of the Amazon, which roughly follows the line of the equator from its source in the Andes to its mouth on the Atlantic, close to the spot where the Portuguese navigator Pedro Álvares Cabral claimed Brazil for his country in 1500. The rest of the country is basically a huge plateau, rising to a maximum height of about 3,000 metres, but with an average altitude of only 500 metres.

What Brazil lacks in extremes of relief, it makes up for in the scale of its natural features. Its coastline measures more than 7,000 kilometres and could almost have been created by

nature as a playground for the ubiquitous Brazilian cult of the body beautiful, since it provides all the great port cities of Belém, Recife, Rio de Janeiro, Salvador and Santos with magnificent beaches at which to swim, surf or simply take the sun.

Connecting the interior to the sea are extensive river systems, of which the longest wholly in Brazil is actually the São Francisco, which loops for 2,900 kilometres through the arid north-eastern heartland to the temperate south-east. It is known as the "river of national unity" because it brings together the four corners of Bra-

zil. In the south, the rivers which form the River Plate system—the Paraguay, Uruguay and Paraná, the third longest river of the Americas—partly flow through Brazil.

But it is the Amazon which seizes the imagination—the greatest river in the world, rivalling the Nile in length and carrying at least 50 times its volume, flowing for more than 6,000 kilometres through the world's largest rainforest. Brazil's timber reserves are the world's third largest, after the Soviet Union and Canada, three quarters of which are found in Amazonia, whose forests—spread like a vast green *bouclé* carpet over three million square kilometres—boast 400 species of hardwood alone. Among them are jacarandas, mahogany and the brazilwood tree, which the first Portuguese colonists exploited for its dye, and which has given its name to the country.

Brazil's other natural resources include immense mineral wealth. It is the world's largest source of aquamarines, topazes, bauxite and niobium. It has gold reserves of 33,000 tonnes, and iron ore deposits estimated at 33 billion tonnes of almost 66 per cent pure iron; it has the world's fourth largest deposits of manganese and the fifth largest of uranium. Enough oil has been found offshore to supply all the country's needs by the 1990s. Agriculture, the original basis of Brazil's wealth, is still an important source of export earnings, employing 30 per cent of the total work force and earning nearly 40 per cent of export income. Brazil is the world's largest producer and exporter of coffee and sugar cane, the second largest of cocoa; it also exports soya beans, tobacco and fruits. In the 1980s, Brazil overtook the U.S. as the leading exporter of orange juice.

But Brazil's most vital resource is its people. With more than 130 million, of which nearly 65 per cent are under 30, it is the sixth most populous nation on earth, and one of the fastest growing, having doubled its population between 1960 and 1985. There is no such thing as a "typical" Brazilian, for virtually every part of the world has contributed at least some share to the genetic pool. A Brazilian might be descended from European settlers, Amerindian natives, African blacks, Asian immigrants—or any combination of these.

Although Brazilians are proud of their reputation as a melting-pot society in which there is a high degree of racial tolerance, most of them recognize four "colour" groups in the population—whites, mainly of European ancestry, who form nearly 62 per cent of the population; browns, mostly of mixed-blood descent, who constitute 27 per cent of Brazilians; blacks, the descendants of Negro slaves, who account for 11 per cent of the total; and yellows, almost entirely the descendants of Japanese immigrants, who make up less than 1 per cent.

In fact, miscegenation has been such a feature of Brazilian society that these distinctions are too blurred to have much significance. They reflect social and economic status rather than racial origins. By and large, the whiter a Brazilian's skin, the greater his opportunities and the higher his social standing; "whiteness" is determined as much by a person's job, clothes, education and manner as by skin colour, so that a wealthy well-educated businessman or woman will be regarded as a "white" regardless of his or her skin colour. Ironically, the one group that *have* been—and to an extent, still are—the victims of racial prejudice, represent the purest strain in Brazilian society—the 200,000 or so Indians of the rainforests.

Despite the size of the population, Brazil is one of the more sparsely settled parts of the globe, with an average of only 15 people per square kilometre, compared with 25 in the United States. Moreover, the population is very unevenly distributed, with more than 90 per cent of it concentrated along the coastal strip, and with only 4 per cent scattered through the Amazon basin, which occupies nearly half the country. Even more striking are the

Skyscrapers dwarf pink-blossomed shrubs in central São Paulo *(left)*, **Brazil's largest city and the hub of the country's economy. Although it had only 31,000 inhabitants a century ago, today the city teems with more than eight million people, of richly diverse ethnic origins** *(above)*.

1

contrasts in living standards between the people in different parts of the country. In the industrialized south, for example, the level of personal income is three times higher than it is in the north-east, where almost one seventh of the population have neither permanent jobs nor land. In a city like Brasília, more than 90 per cent of households have electricity and mains water; in rural regions of the north, 90 per cent or more do not.

Disparities like these fall into a marked regional pattern, recognized by the Brazilian authorities themselves. The authorities have assigned the country's 23 federal states and three territories to five much larger regions, each of which embraces areas that roughly share economic or agricultural problems. Others distinguish six regions: the north-east coast; the arid north-east *sertão*, or backlands; the industrialized south-east, centred on Rio and São Paulo; the mixed farming region of the south; the centre-west; and the north, which includes most of the Amazon basin.

Each of these six regions is distinguished not only by climate and relief, but also by the historical patterns of settlement and economic development based on some primary product— sugar in the north-east coast, coffee and gold in the south-east, rubber in the Amazon. Furthermore, each region has evolved in comparative isolation, with virtually no contact with its neighbours, which lends support to the view that "Brazil is a continent with its colonies inside it".

The oldest of these colonies is the fertile strip of the north-east coast, a "great wild, untidy, luxuriant hothouse" according to the naturalist Charles Darwin, who visited the region in the 1830s. The colony's first export was brazilwood, which was traded from the settlements around Recife, but by the middle of the 16th century the timber trade had been eclipsed by the lucrative sugar industry. For a century north-eastern Brazil enjoyed a virtual world monopoly of the industry, which was centred on Salvador, the country's first capital. Even today, the splendid and numerous 17th-century churches and public buildings attest to the former wealth of the colony, and Salvador, which is usually referred to as Bahia, the name of the state of which it is the capital, has become an important cultural centre with a thriving colony of artists and writers who believe Salvador to be the country's most quintessentially Brazilian city. The sugar industry still plays an important role in the local and national economy for, in addition to traditional food products, it provides the alcohol that now helps to power 40 per cent of the country's vehicles.

The north-east coast is also the region where the cultures of Europe and Africa first came together. Music, dance, religion, language, literature— the whole social and cultural fabric of the nation—have been decisively influenced by the roughly five million Negro slaves who were shipped from Africa to work on the sugar plantations. Although Brazil was the last Western country to abolish slavery— in 1888—there were few taboos on mixed marriages, and many of the plantation owners took black mistresses. The resulting infusion of African culture is very palpable today in the towns and cities of the north-east, where dark faces predominate, where women dress in West African-style swathes of bright cloth, and where the samba, derived from African rhythms, blares from loudspeakers in the street. According to the distinguished writer Jorge Amado, Africa's contribution to the Brazilian character was crucial. "The black man," he says, "has saved us from melancholy and sadness."

On the plateau above the north-eastern coastal strip, the harsh face of tropical Brazil is manifest. This is the north-eastern *sertão*, or backlands— "one of the poorest places on earth" according to the British journalist James Cameron, who added that it was "known as the land of *miseria morte*: the sorrows of death". The *sertão* was first settled as a cattle-raising region, supplying the coastal sugar plantations, but it has never prospered. It is a giant dust bowl—900,000 square kilometres of arid savannah, scrub forests, cactus and thorn bushes, which have been stricken by drought every eight to 15 years, and then devastated by floods. In 1984, for example, a five-year drought ended in torrential rains that left 150 people dead or missing and 700,000 homeless.

Of the 35 million people who live in the region, the most distinctive are the *vaqueiros*, the north-eastern versions of the Brazilian cowboy, who drive their scrawny cattle huge distances in search of pasture. Other inhabitants of the region practise subsistence farming or collect wild gums and waxes that are used in paint and varnish manufacture. But many people have to migrate to earn a living, spending two or three years working on major civil engineering projects all over the country, or find jobs as construction workers in the burgeoning cities of the south-east, where they often live in the buildings they are erecting. Yet they tend to be

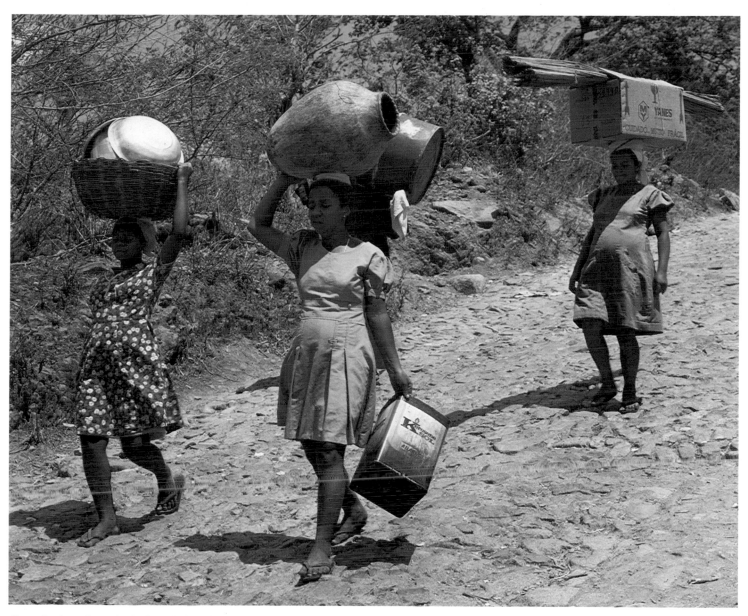

fiercely loyal to their harsh land, and most return when they have saved enough money or hear that the rains are falling again at home.

While all but a handful of sugar plantation owners in the north-east have never known wealth, 1,000 kilometres further south the outward signs of prosperity are very apparent in the huge and modern cities of Rio de Janeiro and São Paulo. Their wealth was founded on gold discovered in the hills of the eastern highlands, 300 kilometres inland from the coast. The precious metal was discovered at the end of the 17th century and so touched off Brazil's second boom, attracting hundreds of thousands of prospectors to Ouro Prêto, a town that derived its name, "Black Gold", from the fact that the gold found in its mines turned black on exposure to the air, owing to the presence of silver in the lode. The state in which most of the discoveries were made was named simply Minas Gerais, "General Mines".

During much of the 18th century, the mines of Minas Gerais provided nearly half the world's annual output of gold, in addition to a total of three million carats of diamonds. With their new-found wealth, the gold miners and merchants turned Ouro Prêto into the finest city in the colony, with 100,000 inhabitants at the height of its prosperity, and with splendid baroque churches, graceful public squares and fountains, and elegant private homes decorated with statuary. Sometimes, though, the new rich of Minas Gerais spent their money on extravagances: one man, for example, built an artificial lake on which he launched a sailing ship so that his mulatta slave girl, who had never travelled by sea, could savour the experience.

By the beginning of the 19th century, however, the gold deposits were nearly exhausted, and by 1821 an English traveller reported that Ouro Prêto "scarcely retains a shadow of its former splendour". Today, with a population of approximately 25,000, Ouro Prêto is a national monument—a major tourist attraction for Brazilians who come to admire their baroque heritage and to examine the square where Brazil's first revolutionary martyr, Joaquim José da Silva Xavier, is commemorated. Known as *Tiradentes*, the "toothpuller", because he was a part-time dentist, Xavier was hanged and quartered in Rio de Janeiro in 1789 for leading a conspiracy against Portuguese colonial rule.

Minas Gerais is still endowed with a great store of mineral wealth, including a mountain so rich in iron that cars and trucks crossing it have to drop a gear and accelerate in order to overcome the magnetic force that impedes their progress. Some of the local ore is processed at Belo Horizonte, the capital of Minas Gerais since 1897, and now a city of two million, producing wagons, tractors, cement, textiles, shoes and foodstuffs.

One of the few towns in the southeast that weathered the collapse of the gold boom was Rio de Janeiro itself. Established as the gateway to the mining regions, it soon assumed such importance that in 1763 it replaced Salvador as the capital, doubling in size to 120,000 inhabitants in the next 10 years. When the gold mines had been exhausted, Rio was perfectly positioned to take advantage of the country's next great economic boom—coffee. The hilly, fertile land behind the capital was ideal for cultivating the coffee shrub, which takes only three to five years to reach maturity and goes on producing abundantly for over 30 years. By 1810, coffee plantations were spread throughout the state of Rio de Janeiro as well as Minas Gerais; by 1830, Brazil was producing over 40 per cent of the world supply; and by 1870, coffee had become the country's most important product.

But one suspects that Rio would have survived and prospered even without the coffee. The city "has edged in between the hills and the sea," wrote the English traveller Peter Fleming, "and on that boldly chosen strip of land has met and trounced the jungle. She gleams up at you complacently, a successful opportunist."

Rio ranks as one of the two or three most beautiful cities in the world, with a natural setting surpassing even Hong Kong and San Francisco. Nestling between blue-green mountains and the turquoise sea, the city stretches for more than 20 kilometres along a magnificent bay whose 16 beaches are interrupted here and there by huge domes of rock which have been worn to pebble roundness by the passage of geological time.

Visitors accustomed to less theatrical cityscapes may find about Rio an

At the Iguaçu Falls, where the borders of Brazil, Argentina and Paraguay meet, some 1,750 cubic metres of water pour over the 60-metre precipice every second. On a visit to Brazil, American First Lady Eleanor Roosevelt said this cluster of 275 cataracts made Niagara Falls look like a kitchen faucet.

air of unreality. "The hand of nature (powerfully aided by the hand of man) stuns new arrivals into a sort of happy dream where anything may happen," wrote Philip Guedalla, the English writer. "Suburban streets end suddenly against the grey flank of a lonely mountain that has somehow got forgotten in a residential neighbourhood; roads climb out of a shopping district into the dripping silence of a forest in the tropics, where the big lianas hang and unimagined flowers blaze in the shadow of the trees, and drivers of oncoming traffic are apt to be bewildered by enormous blue butterflies flapping slowly towards them; and a road-tunnel full of trams opens incredibly upon the sudden blue of unexpected bays that curve between a line of big Atlantic rollers and a tall plantation where the palms are full of enthusiasts watching American football."

Rio's theatrical air is overwhelming during the Carnival celebrations—the annual public madness that goes on continuously from the preceding Friday to the morning of Ash Wednesday. Originally a Catholic religious festival, Carnival has been transformed by a vigorous infusion of African energy into an activity symbolic of everything the world regards as quintessentially Brazilian—beautiful women, dashing men, outrageous costumes and sexual high jinks, the whole thing moving to the rhythm of the samba.

To the thousands of foreign tourists who visit Rio each year, the less appealing aspects of the city are not readily apparent. They do not have to contend every day with the monumental traffic jams, the consequence of its mountain-choked topography and population of five million. To visitors moving between the beaches and the elegant shopping complexes of the high-rise centre, the pastel-coloured *favelas* clustered on the mountainsides may seem picturesque, even romantic, especially during the run-up to Carnival, when the throb of practising samba drummers mingles with the workaday sounds of the city.

In reality, the *favelas*, which house almost a quarter of Rio's population, are noisome slums, in which only a tiny proportion of households have running water, sewage facilities or electricity. In the absence of public medical facilities, or unemployment benefit for the 30 to 40 per cent out of work in the *favelas*, social problems multiply. For these inhabitants of Brazil's "Third World", the glittering "First World" spread out below them is a place experienced only during the frenetic days of Carnival, or through the television in the corner bar, or through crime. Every day there are between 400 and 500 hold-ups in Rio, and visitors are constantly advised about the areas or streets or times of day in which it is unsafe to be abroad.

Year by year the *favelas* continue to grow as landless peasants exchange the grinding poverty of the countryside for urban squalor. Indeed, one of the most striking phenomena of Brazil is the rapid growth of the cities, which has gone hand in hand with the rapid industrialization of the post-war years. In 1940 only 31 per cent of the population lived in the cities, but by 1970 the figure had risen to 56 per cent, and by 1980 two thirds of the population were city-dwellers.

Brazil's fastest-growing city is São Paulo, 350 kilometres south-west of Rio. Although it was founded as early as 1554, its population was only 31,000 in the 1870s, when coffee planters began to move into the region. By 1885 the region had supplanted the state of Rio de Janeiro as the centre of coffee production, and by 1920 São Paulo's population had risen to over half a million. Four years later it overtook Rio as the most important industrial centre in Latin America, although it was not until the 1960s that its population actually overtook Rio's. At the beginning of that decade the population of São Paulo was about 3.7 million. By the end of the decade it was six million, and it has gone on growing at the rate of 350,000 a year. Today it is the largest city in South America, with a metropolitan population estimated at more than 12 million and a skyscraper skyline reminiscent of Chicago.

Largely due to the availability of hydroelectric power in the south, about half of Brazil's industrial production comes from São Paulo. Another factor in the phenomenal growth of the city is its location 800 metres above sea level, which gives it a pleasant temperate climate that has helped attract many skilled European immigrants, plus 200,000 Japanese. Brazilians like these brag of their spirit and enterprise. They criticize the people of Rio as lazy and unenterprising, and they complain of the social and economic drag of the other regions, citing the Brazilian saying that "Brazil is made up of one locomotive and 20 box cars". São Paulo is, of course, the locomotive, and the other states are the box cars.

Descendants of European immigrants, mainly from Germany and Italy, constitute more than half of the population of the south, which has a greater variety of topography, climate and vegetation than any other Brazilian region. Inland features include the forest-clad valleys of the Paraná and Uruguay rivers, which mark the western boundary of the region; the low, rolling grasslands that extend into Rio Grande do Sul from Uruguay; and evergreen-forested uplands that reach their highest point in Paraná. Unlike regions farther north, the south has never had a society divided between plantation owners and slaves, nor has it had an economic boom and bust. Instead it has grown steadily in prosperity, its wealth based on mixed farming and pampas cattle ranching.

Many of the farmers who emigrated to the south clung to their European heritage, refusing to speak Portuguese and building their homes and barns in a style that reminded them of home. At the outbreak of World War II, at least 75 per cent of the inhabitants of Blumenau, not far from the coastal city of Florianopólis, spoke German, and Nazi propaganda was rife. The Brazilian government responded by prohibiting teaching in any language but Portuguese, and by sending German Brazilian youths to do their national service in the north, where they were forced to learn the national language, and where their views on racial purity were modified by contact with beautiful mulatta women. Nowadays, their descendants are more thoroughly assimilated, but the German language is still widely spoken and still, unofficial-

ly, used in schools. In Blumenau jolly brass bands in Tyrolean hats play for the customers in the *Weinstuben*, which serve local wines.

On the prairie-like pampas in the far south, cattle ranching is the main economic activity. The cowboys in this area are called *gaúchos*, like their Argentine counterparts, and tend to look down on their poorer colleagues, the *vaqueiros* of the north-east. They still wear their traditional gaúcho hats, balloon-pleated trousers and brightly coloured shirts, drink hot maté tea out of a chimarrão gourd and, of course, ride superbly well.

The *gaúchos* are a great draw for tourists, but the region's main scenic

1

attraction is the Iguaçu Falls, near the point where Brazil, Argentina and Paraguay come together. Plunging over a 60-metre precipice are the combined waters of some 30 rivers and streams from the interior of Paraná. During the three flood months beginning in May, the water falls at the rate of more than 13,000 cubic metres per second—almost as much as the River Amazon pours into the sea.

Brazil's fifth region, the centre-west, includes the states of Goiás and Mato Grosso, and the federal district of Brasília. The most uniform of the regions, it is part of the great Brazilian plateau, covered with dense tropical forests in the north and sub-tropical savannah and scrub elsewhere. In size and remoteness it is surpassed only by the Amazon basin to the north; it accounts for 22 per cent of the national territory and has large tracts unexplored even today. But it is also Brazil's fastest-growing region (although its population still represents less than 7 per cent of the total), attracting immigrants from all over the country.

Many of these newcomers head for the developed zones around Brasília and Goiás, which are major mining areas, while others carve out a new life in the virgin bush. Some of these pioneers are gold or diamond prospectors, others small-scale farmers. There are also wealthy ranchers—although some of these are more interested in making a killing in real estate than in raising cattle. These people have created an active frontier zone, complete with cowboys and Indians, prospectors and land speculators, where conflicting interests—especially between homesteaders and ranchers—have ended in gun fights and considerable loss of life.

The north, consisting almost entirely of the Amazon basin, is Brazil's last frontier—a wilderness bigger than India, with a population in 1980 of 7.5 million, giving it a density of 1.3 people per square kilometre, compared to more than 50 people per square kilometre in the south. Near the Colombian and Venezuelan frontiers to the north, there are great stretches of grassy plains, and along the Venezuelan border Brazil's highest mountains rise nearly 3,000 metres, but most of the region is densely forested lowland, veined with great rivers that provided the only highways until the 1960s. "The forest of the Amazons is not merely trees and shrubs," wrote the British writer H. M. Tomlinson. "It is not land. It is another element. Its inhabitants are arborean; they have been fashioned for life in that medium as fishes to the sea and birds to the air. Its green apparition is persistent as the sky is and the ocean."

Contrary to appearances, the land is startlingly infertile and the economy of the region has been geared traditionally to the collection of forest products—chiefly nuts, oils, fine woods, medicinal herbs and wild rubber. Most of Amazonia's small farmers and collectors live along the rivers in houses of thatch or planks built on banks or stilts so that they are above the seasonal flood level. Modern Brazil scarcely impinges on these people. Their Catholicism is strongly laced with Indian customs; illiteracy is more than 60 per cent; and infant mortality is shockingly high. Contact with the outside world is mainly through river traders, who periodically stop at the settlements to exchange the amenities of civilization for forest products. Many such communities live in virtual debt-bondage

Crossing the unpaved roadbed of the Trans-Amazonian Highway, poachers carry the body of a jaguar from the dense rainforest. Hunters supplying the world of fashion with skins and furs often use light aircraft and automatic weapons in the pursuit of their illegal trade.

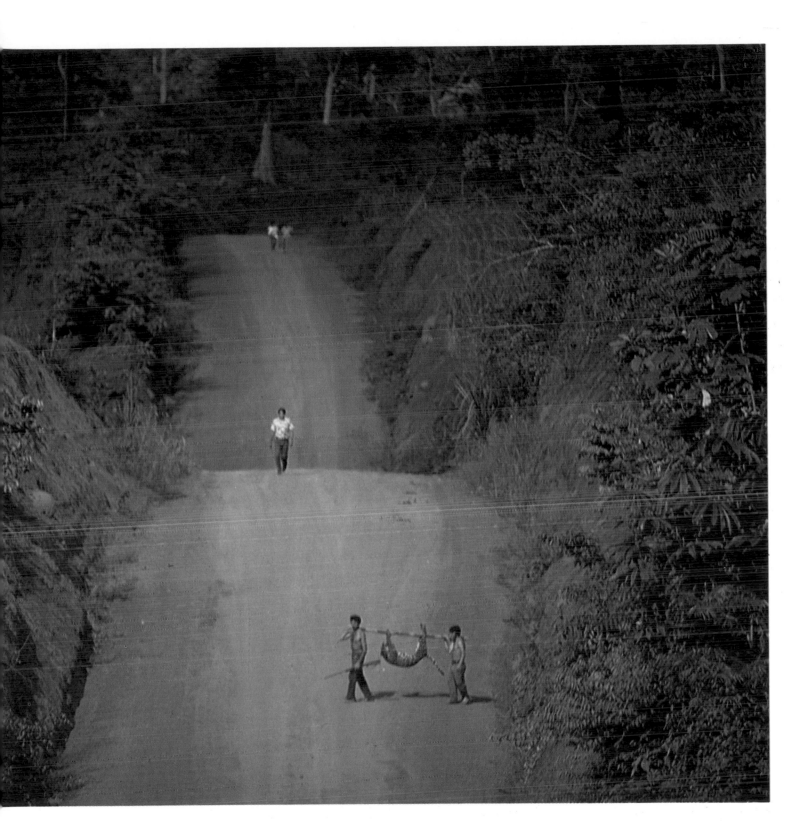

to these river traders, who are themselves often heavily in debt to their suppliers in the towns.

A large proportion of Amazonia's non-Indian population is descended from migrants from the north-east, who settled in the region during a rubber boom which lasted a bare 30 years, from the 1880s. The centre of the market was Manaus, three to five days' journey upriver, which the rubber barons turned into a 19th-century metropolis to vie with Rio. But when the boom went bust the lights of Manaus went out, and the region lapsed into tropical torpor again.

For 40 years Amazonia remained a backwater, but in the 1960s the Brazilian government, worried about the consequences of leaving half their country untenanted, began moves to bring the region into the economic and political mainstream. In 1965 they decided to turn Manaus into a free port, with generous tax incentives, and over the next 15 years the city's fortunes were revived. In the mid-1980s, it had a population of more than 650,000 inhabitants and boasted an important electronics industry.

In order to open up the region, the government financed the construction of the 4,300-kilometre-long Trans-

In a government experimental programme, fast-growing Caribbean pine saplings wait to be planted out in a newly cleared Amazonian woodland. The experiment aims to find a species of tree suitable for wood-pulping that will thrive in the poor forest soils.

Amazonian Highway, from João Pessoa on the Atlantic seaboard right through the rainforest to Peru in the west, together with thousands of kilometres of other trunk roads. Throughout the 1970s, buses streamed down the new highways, carrying migrant smallholders from the *sertão* driven, like their 19th-century predecessors, by the dream of carving out a successful living in the forest. The large-scale settlement of Amazonia is a contentious issue however—partly because farms and ranches that replace trees often have to be abandoned within a few years, victims of the poor soils, and partly because of fears that this unique environment, with the greatest collection of plants and animals on earth, will be destroyed forever.

The miracle of Brazil is that, huge and variegated as it is, with a population whose lifestyles vary dramatically from extreme wealth to dismal poverty, it is a unified country. Even given the contrasting fortunes of its regions, Brazil is one of the few great nations untroubled by separatist factions or regional autonomy movements. Despite the glaring economic gap between town and country, and between slum-dwellers and their wealthy urban neighbours, there is remarkably little enthusiasm for Communism or revolutionary socialism. Despite the widely different ethnic backgrounds of the population and the long years of division into a "slave" class and a "gentleman" class, there is a strong feeling among Brazilians of all racial origins that they form one people and one nation. Brazil, in short, is a paradox of one-ness enclosing many differences.

To an extent, unity has been imposed on the nation by a remarkable uniformity in the administrative and political structure of the disparate regions of the country. Brazil is a federal republic with a constitution based on that of the United States. It grants many powers to the legislatures of its 23 states, which have the right to deal with all matters affecting provincial administration and finance. Much political argument revolves round the relative powers of the federal government and the state legislatures. Nevertheless, from the Amazon rainforest to the southern pampas, state and municipal governments conform to the same system of education, public health, finance and other services.

Under the constitution of 1969, the federal Congress consists of a 69-member Senate and a 479-member Chamber of Deputies. The Senate is two thirds directly elected and one third indirectly elected, while the Chamber of Deputies is elected by universal franchise. This franchise, however, was limited by a literacy qualification which effectively disenfranchised 40 per cent of the population. It was only in 1985 that the literacy requirement was abolished and Brazil became truly democratic.

Democratic government has been suspended several times by both direct and indirect intervention of the military authorities, who have always regarded themselves as guarantors of the Brazilian constitution. But, by the standards of other South American countries, the coups that toppled elected governments were relatively bloodless, and the military regimes that took over were comparatively unrepressive. In 1985, after 21 years of military rule, major constitutional reforms were promised, to meet a popular demand for direct participation at all levels of government, and, possibly, a devolution of powers from the federal government to the states.

National unity, however, does not stem from political institutions alone, and the lack of friction between the elements is due to a number of historical factors. The kings of Portugal, often because they lacked the resources and power to impose their will, ruled Brazil in a tolerant fashion that left the colonists room to develop in their own fashion. Historically, too, the Portuguese language and the Catholic Church were crucial unifying factors. Portuguese Catholicism, never as exigent as the Church in Spanish South America, proved as malleable as the colonial power. From Brazil's early days, for example, it took a permissive view of the sexual morals of the Portuguese settlers towards African and Indian women, and so opened the door to the great mixture of races that has become the Brazilian nation. Equally, after an initial attempt to suppress the religions brought to Brazil by the African slaves, the Church came to tolerate them, and even absorbed African religious practices and gods into its own liturgy and family of saints.

This was a major consideration in a nation which claims to be the largest Catholic community in the world, since it gave Brazil a cultural matrix that could be applied to all the various regions and peoples of the emerging nation. The new nation is certainly, as Jorge Amado says, "a hybrid nation, a hybrid people with a hybrid culture", but Brazil nevertheless has a unity which is unmistakable. It is that unity which makes him add: "What gives me confidence in Brazil, is our capacity not to give in to poverty and oppression, but to fight and go forward."

THE BEACH AS A WAY OF LIFE

With 7,408 kilometres of white sands strung out along the Atlantic seaboard, and temperatures that rarely fall below 20°C, the beaches of Brazil are an irresistible magnet for anyone within reach of the coast. Pulsing with life, throbbing with samba music, the curving shores and palm-fringed inlets are a meeting place for all races and classes. Bronzing in their scanty bikinis, young girls from the shanty towns lie down as equals alongside heiresses from the glittering towers of Copacabana. Businessmen in swimsuits stroll along, wheeling and dealing, as the ripples lap at their feet, barely noticing the volleyball players, the skin-divers or the schoolchildren sprawled out doing their homework on the sand.

For some people, the beach is a marketplace, a bazaar of balloons, costume jewellery, and ice creams flavoured with exotic tropical fruits. For others, it is a source of life itself: the shellfish which are gathered at low tide nourish families without enough money to buy such delicacies in the shops.

The beach remains busy long after sunset. The sands become a dance floor, a lovers' trysting spot, or a place for prayer—on certain nights, devotees of the spiritist cults that first arrived with the African slave ships meet here to honour the deities of the sea.

So integral are beaches to the national way of life that, for many Brazilians, a town is only as good as its proximity to the sands and the surf. The lucky residents of Rio de Janeiro, with its 80 kilometres of strand, or of Salvador, with its turquoise bay and tranquil lagoons, feel only pity for the 65 per cent of the Brazilian population who live inland, far from the sight or sound of the sea.

At Boca do Rio, outside Salvador, swimmers are undeterred by a turbulent surf, whipped up by stormy autumn winds. The tall trees on the dunes are among the 40 different species of coconut palm native to the coast of Brazil, once known to the Indians as the "Land of Palms".

Wearing the scantiest of bikinis, known as *tangas*, two sunlovers soak up the rays on Rio de Janeiro's Copacabana Beach. Some 100,000 *Cariocas*—citizens of Rio—flock to the fashionable Copacabana each weekend, although it is just one of a dozen beaches that serve Brazil's most hedonistic city.

Against a setting of brilliant sand and wooded dunes, local women do their washing and bathe their children while a fisherman tries his luck in the dark waters of the Lagoa do Abaeté. The freshwater lagoon, celebrated in folksongs and paintings, lies 30 kilometres inland from Salvador.

On Ribeira Beach, near Salvador, coast-dwellers take advantage of the low tide to dig the exposed mud flats for clams and mussels. For the poorest households, this daily harvest of shellfish is a vital source of protein, free for the taking.

A hat-seller strides along Copacabana Beach carrying aloft an umbrella that supports an eye-catching display of headgear and dangling bottles of suntan lotion. Behind him, white-coated vendors hawk cold drinks from metal drums.

On Copacabana Beach, in the shadow of Sugar Loaf Mountain, a young football player defends the goal. Professional league teams stage free matches on the sands on Saturdays; during the rest of the week youthful fans meet here to emulate their heroes.

41

The earliest accurate chart of Brazil,
produced in 1519, shows the
Portuguese flag flying north of the
River Amazon *(top left-hand corner)* and
south of the River Plate. Indians are
depicted chopping and gathering logs
of the brazilwood tree which gave its
name to the new-found country.

QUESTS AND CONQUESTS

On March 9, 1500, an expedition of 13 ships and 1,200 men under the command of Admiral Pedro Álvares Cabral set sail from Lisbon, Portugal, bound for India via the sea route newly established by the trail-blazing navigator, Vasco da Gama. Six weeks later the look-outs in the fleet reported sightings of weeds and reeds in what they presumed to be mid-ocean, and two days later they were astonished to spy land to the westward at latitude 17° South. In this way was Brazil, now the greatest country of South America, and the fifth largest nation on earth, "discovered" in the west by sailors who were supposed to be sailing to the east.

Nobody knows for sure why Cabral's fleet, supposedly skirting Africa, should have strayed so far off course that it fetched up in South America. Some suggest that it was the result of high winds or an egregious navigational error; others maintain that westward exploration was Cabral's secret intention all along. Nor is it at all evident that the Portuguese were the first Europeans to "discover" Brazil; both the French and the Spanish have staked strong prior claims. Nevertheless, Cabral's arrival on April 22, 1500, is taken as the moment of birth for Brazil, and the letter subsequently written to the King of Portugal by his ship's chronicler, Pero Vaz de Caminha, is recognized as the first official account of the new-found land.

Caminha's letter describes, in commendable detail and with barely restrained excitement, what the Portuguese sailors encountered when they landed at the mouth of a forested river near present-day Porto Seguro, between Bahia and Rio de Janeiro. Native Indians were already on the beach to meet them as they drew near in a longboat, Caminha related. "They were dark and entirely naked, with nothing to cover their private parts, and carried bows and arrows in their hands. Nicolau Coelho made a sign to them to lay down their bows, and they laid them down. He could not speak with them there because of the breaking of the sea on the shore."

After the Portuguese had landed, the white men and the natives were touchingly friendly towards one another. The Indians danced to the lilt of the Portuguese bagpipes in a forest clearing, and later, when two of the Indian chiefs visited Cabral's flagship and fell asleep on the deck, the sailors spread a cloak over their bodies and put pillows under their heads. It is one of the great tragedies of Brazilian history that such promising cordiality between the two races was to be such a brief interlude in their centuries of contact and interwoven development.

Cabral's expedition spent only nine more days exploring the coast of Brazil before setting a proper course for India. But during their short stay the Portuguese did two things of great symbolic significance for the future of colonialism in Brazil. One act was to hold a Christian service at which they persuaded the Indians to kneel before a huge wooden cross. The other was to leave behind two convicts under sentence of death. The Portuguese viewed miscegenation as a major step to colonization, and so Cabral had brought along convicts to be left to interbreed with the natives of any suitable land encountered. The two stranded men wept in vain on the shore as the fleet weighed anchor. Then they settled down to a lifetime of procreation—the first of thousands upon thousands of Portuguese who were to change the human mix in Brazil beyond recognition.

Cabral had christened the newly discovered country *Terra da Vera Cruz*—the Land of the True Cross. But within a few years it was popularly known as Brazil, named after the brazilwood tree which soon became much sought-after in Europe for the valuable, rich red dye that was extracted from its wood. The name *Terra do Brasil*, the Land of the Brazilwood Tree, first appeared on a map in 1511; and for a few score years brazilwood was almost the only commodity of economic interest to come out of the country. At this time the Portuguese were far more concerned with developing their spice trade in the Far East. But by the late 1520s, that trade had dwindled dramatically; and so, more and more, they turned their attention to the economic potentials of Brazil.

The Portuguese began sending ships to patrol the Brazilian coast and fend off French and Dutch intruders. When this failed to discourage foreign rivals, they decided to found a major colony. In 1531 Admiral Martim Alfonso de Sousa was sent out with five ships, 400 sailors and colonists, and seeds, plants

2

and domestic animals. The following year he founded the coastal settlement of São Vicente near present-day Santos, and on order of his king, João III, he divided Brazil into 15 "captaincies", or districts, marked out at roughly 250-kilometre intervals along the coast, and stretching far into the unexplored interior. Each district was granted in perpetuity to a person prominent in the Portuguese court—a feudal practice which guaranteed that the land would be colonized without expense to the royal exchequer.

Initially, the captaincies developed feebly. The distances were enormous and communications so difficult that the territories suffered from extreme isolation. They also suffered from lack of funds and lack of people. The major crop was sugar cane, along with wheat and grape vines; numerous colonists also tried cattle ranching. Many plantations failed, however, while some succeeded only to be destroyed by hostile Indians or French interlopers. Portugal's Brazilian colony demanded stronger direction, and so, in 1549, the King sent out the first Governor General, Tomé de Sousa, to co-ordinate the development and defence of the captaincies. He was accompanied by Jesuit priests who were to look after the religious interests of the colonies and evangelize the Indians.

The new Governor General established his administration at the new town of Salvador, strategically placed midway between the far north and the far south of the country. Thereafter, new settlements sprang up in rapid succession—most notably São Paulo, founded in 1554, and Rio de Janeiro, which was established in 1565 in response to an abortive French attempt to found a colony on the shores of Guana-

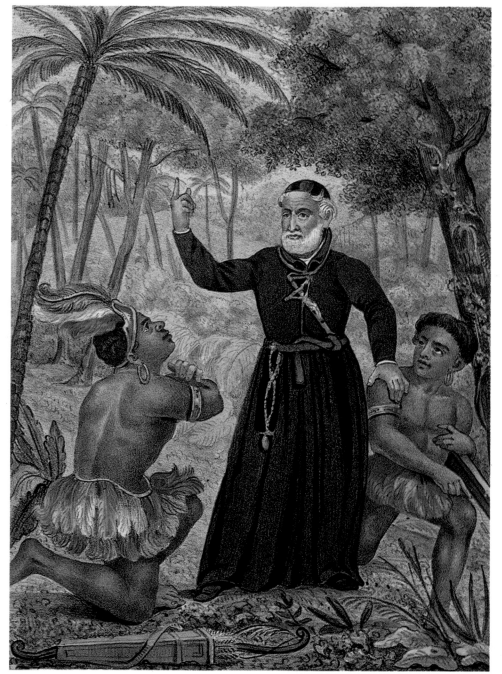

44

bara Bay. The white population of the colony increased from 3,000 in 1549 to 20,000 in 1570. Meanwhile, increasingly huge tracts of land were given over to the cultivation of sugar cane, especially in Pernambuco, Bahia and São Vicente, and, within a decade, Brazil had become the leading sugar-producing region in the world.

Sugar plantations were voracious establishments; their appetite for land, capital and labour was seemingly insatiable. In Brazil, land abounded and capital could generally be found, but labour was scarce. There were not enough white settlers, and anyway they were not much inclined towards hard labour. The obvious solution was to press the native population into forced labour. Many Indian tribes resisted, and invariably at terrible cost as the European invaders replied with a long succession of campaigns of extermination or pacification.

The coastal tribes were the first victims of this protracted holocaust. The warlike Tupinambá tribe around Rio de Janeiro and Bahia were virtually liquidated by slaughter, slavery and confinement in Jesuit missions. In Pernambuco, the Caeté were wiped out by military expeditions, and, far and wide, entire villages were eliminated by European epidemic diseases such as smallpox, measles and influenza, against which the Indians had no immunity. During the 17th century, the Indians of the interior suffered the same fate as a consequence of repeated slave-hunting expeditions.

Until they were expelled from Brazil in 1759, the Jesuits attempted to protect the Indians from the ravages of the slave hunters. They settled them in special villages where they could be christianized and taught trades useful to colonial society. But outside the Jesuit villages the Indians continued for many more years to be rounded up and pressed into forced labour on plantations where they never remained long in service, dying either of disease or the death-wish, or running away to join Indian tribes hostile to whites. There were at least two million Indians in Brazil when the Portuguese first arrived (some estimates put the figure as high as five million), but in less than a century probably two thirds of them had been liquidated.

Statistically, the reduction in numbers among the indigenous Indians of Brazil was more or less balanced by the import of slaves from Portugal's African colonies in Guinea and Angola. From the middle of the 16th century, slave shipments arrived regularly for sale to sugar-cane growers. Many slaves died on the crossing, chained like animals in pestilential holds that reached furnace heat in the tropical climate. Some 30,000 Africans were estimated to have been brought in during the remainder of the 16th century, half a million during the following century, and a grand total of up to 3.3 million by the time the slave trade was abolished in 1850, more than 300 years after it had begun.

The African slaves were very much stronger and harder workers than their Indian counterparts; they were also more resistant to disease. Their presence in the plantations of the north worked wonders in terms of increased production and profits. In the south, however, plantation owners were generally unable to afford the high asking price for African slaves, and so they continued to exploit native Indian labour. But, black or brown, slaves were literally worked to death—or simply murdered by sadistic owners. It was not unknown for slaves to be boiled alive in the sugar vats or castrated with a razor as a punishment for some misdemeanour or other.

In Brazil, there were several harvests of cane during the year, so there was scarcely any period when slaves were unprofitably idle. "A sugar mill is hell," reported the Jesuit Andrés de Gouvea in 1627, "and all the masters are damned." Like so many visitors to Brazilian sugar mills, he was appalled by the nightmarish scenes presented by the roaring furnaces, the bubbling cauldrons and the eternal grinding of the mill machinery, which worked continuously, day and night.

The world of the sugar plantation was a microcosm of early colonial Brazil. Within it, the slaves represented the rock bottom of the social order, while the white planters were its aristocracy. The wealthy sugar captains generally lived on their vast estates in the *casas grandes*, or great houses, and below them lay the cane fields, the mills, the quarters of the white and coloured artisans, and the barracks, or *senzalas*, of the slaves. But while the Brazilian whites controlled every facet of the black slaves' lives, the sheer numbers of the slaves profoundly influenced the formation of Brazilian society and transformed the physiognomy of the people. From the very beginning the Portuguese settlers had been partial to the naked Indians, and they found the African blacks equally attractive. Slave concubines became the norm rather than the exception. The Church and polite society looked the other way. There was a great need to populate the country, so all procreation was seen as a contribution to the greater cause. Many white fathers felt inclined to free their half-white offspring, along with their black mothers, so before long a considerable number of free non-whites began to take their place in Brazilian society.

Throughout the 17th century, Brazil's wealth was centred in the north-east, where the largest and most productive sugar plantations were situated. The south, by contrast, remained relatively undeveloped and, as a result, it was the southern Brazilians who were driven by economic necessity to make the most determined and daring efforts to explore deep into the interior. In doing so they were largely responsible for the westward advancement of Brazil's frontiers, and in the end they were to provide the means that made possible the colony's rapid development. They discovered gold.

The pioneers who blazed the trail into the interior were the so-called *bandeirantes*—the epic heroes of Brazil, tough, intrepid, rapacious members of armed bands, who set off into the untrodden wilderness beyond the coastal fringe in search of Indian slaves and precious stones and metals. The *bandeirantes* (literally "flag-bearers") were soldiers of fortune, mainly Paulistas—settlers of São Paulo. They drew into their ranks backwoodsmen from every shade of Brazil's racial mix, especially men of mixed Amerindian blood.

In a different land and a different age they might well have won praise as outstanding figures in the history of geographical exploration. They travelled enormous distances on foot or by canoe. They penetrated the mountain barriers, cut trails through the bush, followed the turbulent rivers of the vast forests, waded the swamps, pressed on across the parched scrub drylands, always forward into forbidding regions no outsider had seen before. But these explorers were mainly illiterate, anonymous men who left few traces in the geographical records. Wearing loose cotton trousers, a broad-rimmed hat and little else, the *bandeirante* was a veritable walking arsenal—a sword and pistol in his belt, a bow in his hand, a knife hanging from his chest, a rifle over his shoulder and cartridge belts round his body. He survived by mastering the bushcraft of the Indian, and became inured to hunger, thirst, fatigue and the hostility of the insects and climate. Warlike Indian tribes learned to fear such intruders.

By the early 18th century, the major settlements of Brazil had been linked by a communications network pioneered by the *bandeirantes*. Fleets of 20-metre-long dugout canoes plied the rivers. Mule trains, with as many as 50 mules, operated regular trading schedules across bush and mountains, and, in the process, the *bandeirantes* not only opened up the country, but helped to unify it as well. They pacified or enslaved the Indian tribes that barred westward progress, and by their discoveries of gold they initiated the most dramatic phase in the development of their country.

Between 1693 and 1695 discoveries of alluvial gold were made in valleys of the region that is now the south-central state of Minas Gerais ("General Mines"). Adventurers and vagabonds from all over the colony joined in the subsequent gold rush, and before long fleets of fortune-seekers were arriving from Europe, too. The human flood—one without parallel until the California gold rush of 1849—continued for years, even though the land journey to the farthest gold strikes could take seven months or more and was perilous in the extreme. One route, for example, involved negotiating a hundred rapids, and there was always great loss of life when canoes overturned. Hostile Indians also exacted their toll, one tribe killing 600 men in a single convoy and more than 400 men in another.

Conditions in the remote, undeveloped region of the gold fields were lawless and tumultuous, and for the first decade or so the miners were beyond the control of the colonial government. Indeed, the conflicts between rival groups of miners sometimes erupted into outright warfare. Yet the flood of dreamers of eldorado continued for decades. Boom towns sprang up overnight, and some miners' camps grew into miniature cities, dazzling outposts of 18th-century culture.

The lifestyle in these towns was one of enormous contrasts. The few who struck it rich were wildly ostentatious spenders. "They went about accompanied by troops of matchlock men," reported the Italian Jesuit, Antonil, "ready to execute any violence and to take the greatest and most frightful revenge, without any fear of the law. The gold excited them to gamble lavishly, and heedlessly to squander vast sums on vain luxuries. For instance, they would give one thousand *cruzados* for a Negro Trumpeteer; and double that for a mulatto prostitute, in order to indulge with her in continual and scandalous sins." On the other hand, luckless prospectors suffered appalling hardships in an infertile region where food prices were more than 50 times higher than those on the coast.

The gold rush played havoc with the economy of Brazil. Sugar and tobacco plantations in the east were often abandoned in favour of the search for quick riches in the gold fields, and foodstuffs, goods, cattle, slaves and services gravitated to the mining settlements. Meanwhile, the government was unable to suppress the widespread traffic of contraband gold as miners became more and more adept at avoiding payment of the tax called the *quinto* or "royal fifth". They were often abetted in their efforts to do this by delinquent priests who smuggled gold dust to the coast inside hollow crucifixes.

Brazil's output of precious minerals (diamonds as well as gold were eventually discovered in Mato Grosso, Goiás and Minas Gerais) reached a maximum in 1760. By then, nearly half the world's supply of gold was being produced by Brazil. Coming at a time of decline in Portugal's economy, these riches should have provided the Portuguese exchequer with a massive boost. But some of the new wealth was misspent in Lisbon on royal and civic ex-

travagances, and much of the rest went to London to pay off Portugal's mounting deficit in the balance of trade with the English.

In the long term the gold cycle did not enrich either Portugal or Brazil, but, through inflation, contributed to their impoverishment. Indeed, the obsession with gold brought the area of Minas Gerais to the verge of self-destruction; and in the 1770s, when the gold cycle finally declined, only

2

diversification into other economic activities, most notably cattle ranching, enabled the region to survive.

There were, however, some compensations of fundamental importance. The gold rush opened up the interior and it provided a powerful impetus for the urbanization of Brazil. It also stimulated immigration on an unprecedented scale: 400,000 Portuguese left for Brazil in the 18th century, and two million slaves were shipped over from Africa—a third of them destined for the gold mines. By 1725, half the total colonial population was living in the gold region of south-central Brazil, and as a consequence the colony's centre of gravity was shifted from the north-east to the south-east. The result

was that, in 1763, the capital was transferred from Salvador, where it had been for more than 200 years, to Rio de Janeiro.

The move to Rio more or less coincided with the beginning of a period of economic stagnation in Brazil, which was aggravated by the Portuguese authorities. They regarded their Brazilian possession as a milch cow; they put taxes, tithes and duties on all production and commerce, forbade manufacturing and burdened the economy with countless restrictions. Not surprisingly, the Brazilian-born whites deeply resented these impositions, just as, in other parts of the New World, the English-speaking Americans and the creoles of Spanish America re-

sented demands being made by London or Madrid.

In Minas Gerais, resentment simmered for years, culminating in 1789 in the formation of an abortive and tragic independence movement known as the *Inconfidência Mineira*, or Minas Conspiracy, which was composed of poets, priests, landowners, merchants and army officers. The conspiracy was led by Lieutenant Joaquim José da Silva Xavier, a young soldier popularly known as *Tiradentes*, "the toothpuller", because he was also a part-time dentist. The conspirators were greatly inspired by the American Revolution and corresponded with Thomas Jefferson, to whom they looked for support. But the plans of their revolt were exposed; the *Inconfidência* was broken up, and *Tiradentes* was publicly hanged and quartered, his home demolished, and the site strewn with salt to ensure, symbolically, that the land of his roots would be barren forever. Brazil had its first martyr to freedom.

Other abortive *Inconfidências* followed—in Rio in 1794, Bahia in 1798 and Pernambuco in 1801. By now Brazilian feelings had evolved from resentment of economic exploitation to a growing awareness of Brazilian national pride and identity. A few of Brazil's potential revolutionaries were republicans who wished to see the overthrow of the Portuguese Crown. However, the great majority were moderate reformers who simply wished for a better deal for the colonies. In the circumstances, decades might have passed without fundamental change but for the indirect intervention in Brazil's affairs of one supremely ambitious foreigner—Napoleon Bonaparte.

In November 1807, at the height of the Peninsula War, Napoleon's forces marched upon Lisbon. To avoid falling into French hands, the Prince Regent of Portugal (the future King João VI), together with his mad mother, Queen Maria, and 15,000 members of the Portuguese court, boarded a fleet of 40 merchant vessels and, under the protection of British warships, set sail for their colony in Brazil. After a hideous, storm-racked voyage of 54 days, the royal court landed in Salvador, and two months later, amid scenes of tumultuous rejoicing on the part of their Brazilian subjects, arrived in Rio de Janeiro. The Prince Regent at once took over direct rule in place of his viceroy; and so the colonial capital became a royal capital and Rio the *de facto* capital of the Portuguese Empire.

This was a decisive moment in the history of Brazil. Dom João soon fell in love with his country of exile, and in due course he set about transforming it. In Lisbon he had seen the world from the point of view of a Portuguese in Europe. Now his outlook became Brazilianized, or Rio-centric; he began to initiate changes which the Brazilians had proposed and the Portuguese had vetoed for years. His first act was to end nearly three centuries of Portuguese mercantile monopoly by legalizing Brazilian trade with friendly nations and the establishment of manufacturing industries on Brazilian soil. The impact of this was first felt in the capital. In 1808, only 90 foreign ships had anchored at the port of Rio de Janeiro; by 1822, the annual number had risen to 422. Most of the ships now entering Guanabara Bay were British. They brought with them every conceivable product of the Industrial Revolution, together with pushy British businessmen who were eager to exploit a virgin market.

The emporiums of the British merchants in Rio were Aladdin's caves of manufactured goods such as few Brazilians had ever seen, and it was not long before the British lifestyle was modifying that of the Brazilians. In Rio, particularly, the citizens acquired a taste for tea, took to eating their meals with Sheffield cutlery instead of fingers, and garbed themselves in the dark and sober clothing of the bankers and mill owners of cold northern Europe—black frock coats, boots and top hats more appropriate to the London Stock Exchange than to the steaming, palm-fringed, parrot-coloured world along the Tropic of Capricorn.

After the British came the French. Following Napoleon's final eclipse at Waterloo in 1815, they poured into Rio as refugees. Their influence was less materialistic and more hedonistic than that of the British. The French set themselves up as the purveyors of life's little luxuries, selling confections, rich pastries, fine wines, jewels and Paris fashions. They opened the first hotel and introduced the first *à la carte* menu of French *haute cuisine*. At least in its capital, Brazil became a more sophisticated place.

The year the French came was the year Dom João refused to go. After Napoleon's defeat it was expected that he would return with his court to Lisbon. Instead he chose to stay, and then systematically set about hauling his adopted country into the 19th century. He founded the first newspaper, the first bank, the first military and naval academies, the first medical school, theatre, library, museum and observatory. In Rio—now a city of 100,000 people and growing prosperous on coffee, an important new plantation crop for export—he founded the Botanical Gardens and introduced the habit of sea bathing. The streets of the city were paved, illuminated and policed. Brazil was being modernized and Europeanized; inevitably such processes had a profound effect on the political state of the country.

In 1816 Dom João's mad old mother died and the Prince Regent was proclaimed King João VI. Five years later he finally bowed to pressure to return to Portugal, leaving behind his son, Pedro, as Prince Regent. With the Crown again based in the mother country, the Portuguese began blundering efforts to turn back the clock and reduce Brazil to its former dependent colonial status. This arrogance, which culminated in the withdrawal of

In one of Brazil's great moments of history, the Prince Regent, Dom Pedro, raises his sword to cry "Independence or death!", thus signalling Brazil's break from Portugal. The event, captured by the Brazilian artist Pedro Américo, took place on the banks of the Ipiranga river in September 1822.

nearly all the gold reserves in the Bank of Brazil, was countered in the colony with rising nationalist and separatist fervour. For Dom Pedro there was a stark choice: he could head the independence movement or he could lose control of Brazil altogether.

On September 7, 1822—as every Brazilian patriot is taught in his cradle—the Prince Regent, resting on horseback beside a little river called the Ipiranga, in São Paulo, received a fresh batch of typically high-handed orders from Lisbon. He was so angry when he read them that he drew his sabre from its scabbard, brandished it in the air, and let out a fearful shout which has echoed down the generations as the famous *Grito*, or Cry, of Ipiranga. "*Independência ou morte!*" he yelled. "Independence or death!" One month later he was acclaimed Emperor and, on December 1, was crowned in Rio de Janeiro with much pomp and ceremony. So began the era of the independent Brazilian Empire—and a giant step was taken towards the making of the modern nation of today.

Dom Pedro was not well cast in his newly assumed role of Emperor. His personality was too wayward and mercurial, and his private life too scandalous, to befit the solemn grandeur of his office. A dissipated neurotic who suffered from epileptic fits, he scandalized even the broad-minded Brazilians with his amorous indiscretions and his growing litter of bastard children. The Emperor liked to think that he was an avant-garde liberal, and in 1824 he promulgated a constitution which gave him considerable powers but, with a Chamber of Deputies which was indirectly elected on a limited suffrage, was still sufficiently progressive to survive

for the greater part of the 19th century. However, he himself reigned for only nine years. During that time he never succeeded in imposing his will on the country as a whole, and there were endless revolts and mercenary mutinies in the different regions.

In 1831, the first Emperor of Brazil was forced to abdicate in favour of his son, also named Dom Pedro, only five years of age. In 1840, after nine years of regency, the boy, despite his youth, was crowned. It marked the dawn of a new age of political and material development comparable in some ways to another marathon reign just beginning in Queen Victoria's England. The new Emperor, hardworking, liberal and cultivated, was destined to rule for almost half a century. As a constitutional monarch, Dom Pedro II had his authority theoretically limited to what was known as his "moderating power", under which he was allowed to appoint or dismiss any member of the government, prorogue parliament or dissolve the Chamber of Deputies. Importantly, however, he used this power with discretion, appointing the best men for the job regardless of their political persuasions. It can be argued that neither before nor since has Brazil been administered by men of such calibre.

Brazil's material expansion really began during Dom Pedro II's reign. More banks were opened, more foreign capital (mainly British) flowed in for commercial and industrial development. The Emperor himself was keenly interested in scientific advances. He was the first person in Brazil to have his photograph taken, and the first to speak on the telephone. With his encouragement, the railway age was launched in 1859 when the first steam train rumbled out of Rio towards the Emperor's summer residence at Petropolis. In 1874, Dom Pedro himself went down to the beach at Copacabana—then an uninhabited stretch of sand—to inaugurate a submarine cable between Rio and London.

He served his country well for 49 years. Under his enlightened and responsible rule, economic production increased tenfold and public revenues fourteenfold. There was, however, just one major blot on his reign: the continuation of slavery. Dom Pedro personally believed this to be an abomination, but at the same time he was not prepared to sanction its immediate abolition because he feared the economic, social and political consequences.

The slave trade from Africa had been declared illegal in 1831 and was brought to an end in 1850, but there was still no law against the continued ownership of slaves in Brazil. By the 1880s emancipation had become the greatest issue of the age. Many Brazilians were deeply ashamed that theirs was the only Christian nation that still permitted slavery; even the army protested at being ordered to pursue runaways, and several states took the unilateral decision to liberate their slaves. Clearly this 300-year-old institution was doomed. But still the plantation aristocracy would not give way, and still the Emperor delayed.

In 1887, tired and diabetic, the Emperor went to Europe for a holiday.

The abolitionists, headed by Dom Pedro's daughter, Princess Isabel, who was now acting as regent, seized their chance. On May 13, 1888—a quarter of a century after slavery had been abolished in the United States and 55 years after it had been abolished in the British colonies—the Princess signed the "Golden Law", freeing all slaves in Brazil without compensation to their owners.

"You have redeemed a race but lost a crown," the Princess was warned by the landowners. They meant what they said. Some rich planters were ruined, and in their ruin and their wrath they turned against the monarchy and gave their support to a republican movement of middle-class businessmen and

THE AMAZON RIVER'S VORACIOUS PREDATOR

The full menace of the piranha is captured in a drawing *(left)*, taken from a book published in 1829 by the naturalists J. B. de Spix and Louis Agassiz. Among the many vivid descriptions of this freshwater hunter is one by the former U.S. President, Theodore Roosevelt, who visited Amazonia in 1913–14. "The head," he wrote, "with its short muzzle, staring and malignant eyes and gaping, cruelly armed jaws, is the embodiment of cruel ferocity." One species reaches 60 centimetres, but most average 20 to 30. They travel in large shoals and chiefly attack other fish, whose flesh they bite off with sharp, triangular teeth.

Nothing attracts piranha quicker than blood, and an attacking shoal, which can number hundreds of fish, makes short shrift of large wounded animals, or humans. A school of piranha is on record as having reduced a 45-kilogram capybara to a skeleton in under a minute.

disaffected elements of the army who were angry with the Emperor because he insisted they stay out of politics. Unaware of these rumblings, the Emperor returned to Brazil and a warm welcome from the majority of his subjects. But within weeks a conspiracy was hatched by the army against him: on November 15, 1889, a republic was proclaimed and two days later he was sent into exile with his family. In 1891, the country's last Emperor died forlornly but without recrimination in a second-class hotel room in Paris.

Until 1894, the new republic of Brazil was ruled by a provisional government under a military autocracy. It made some crucially important decisions, including the separation of Church and State, and the adoption of a constitution modelled on that of the United States. By the dawn of the 20th century, however, it was becoming clear that the shift to a federal republic and presidential rule had brought about little change in Brazil's basic political and social institutions.

The mass of the people in Brazil remained outside the political process since the suffrage was based on literacy and, of the 20 to 30 per cent of the population thought to be entitled to vote in municipal, state and national elections, only about three per cent bothered to do so. Also, because power had been decentralized to the states, big landowners exercised enormous influence, particularly in the states of São Paulo and Minas Gerais, where the political and economic power was mainly concentrated. Most significantly, the military had become more and more politically active as they asserted their claim as guarantors of the constitutional process and served as a check on civilian administrations.

The most dramatic changes at this time occurred in the agricultural economy. Following the decline in gold mining, coffee began to rival and then overtook sugar cane as the outstanding export crop and source of government revenue. Meanwhile, Brazil was profiting increasingly from a natural resource that had remained untapped until 1839, when the American Charles Goodyear had invented the rubber vulcanizing process. Rubber trees grew wild in great abundance throughout the Amazon valley—an estimated 300 million trees in five million square kilometres of forest. And the demand for rubber increased sharply with the advent of motor cars with rubber tyres.

By the 20th century, the Amazon was providing the rubber for most of the world's cars.

The centre of the rubber boom became Manaus, capital of Amazonas State but until then a small town isolated in the heart of the rainforest 1,600 kilometres upstream from the Atlantic. Yet, by the early 1900s it had grown into one of the grandest and most extravagant places on the whole continent. "I found a village," boasted the State Governor of the time, "and made of it a modern city." Manaus had the first electrified public transport service in South America and the first telephone system in the Amazon. There were hospitals and banks and billiard rooms, a racecourse and a bullring, a Grand Hotel—"the finest in Christendom"—and even a lavishly decorated opera house.

Rubber, quite simply, made Manaus the new Babylon of Brazil. There were nightspots and brothels galore where girls from every country of Europe and the Orient were available at staggering prices. At private parties in the luxurious villas and palaces of the rubber kings, naked girls took showers in iced Cordon Rouge, and on such nights a tycoon thought nothing of lighting a cigar with a 500 milreis note, the equivalent today of over £100. The new rich sent their laundry to Lisbon and their children to smart schools in Switzerland and France. They ordered their marble columns from Italy, their furniture from London, their vegetables from Brussels and their opera singers from Milan.

By the early 1910s, rubber was almost the equal of coffee as Brazil's main earner of foreign currency, and some 5,000 people a week were still swarming into Manaus to seek their

A CHRONOLOGY OF KEY EVENTS

c. 10,000 B.C. Hunter-gatherers from North America reach Brazil. They gradually settle in widely dispersed tribal grounds and develop cultures based on hunting and gathering.

1494 The Treaty of Tordesillas divides the New World—both discovered and undiscovered—between Spain and Portugal.

1500 The navigator Pedro Álvares Cabral *(below)* sights the Brazilian coast and lands to claim the region for Portugal.

1532 Portuguese settlers establish their first colony at São Vicente.

1534 Brazil is divided into 15 captaincies—hereditary land grants later to become administrative units.

1538 The Portuguese start to import African slaves *(below)* to work on their sugar plantations.

1549 The newly founded city of Salvador becomes the seat of colonial government.

1554 The Jesuits found a mission at São Paulo.

1600 Expeditions into the interior by hard-bitten settlers known as *bandeirantes* (flag-bearers) begin to extend Brazil's territory westwards. The *bandeirantes* repeatedly clash with Jesuits attempting to protect the Indians from slavery and exploitation by the settlers.

1639 Portugal claims the Amazon basin.

1654 The expulsion of Dutch settlers from Brazil marks the end of a succession of attempts by other nations—including Britain and France—to gain a share of Portugal's South American discoveries.

1680 Brazil expands southwards to the River Plate and comes into conflict with the Spanish over Uruguay.

1693 Gold is discovered in the Brazilian hinterland and a century-long gold rush begins.

1750 Spain and Portugal settle Brazilian border disputes by the Treaty of Madrid, which supersedes the Treaty of Tordesillas.

1754 Brazil's administrative structure is revised, with the abolition of the hereditary captaincies.

1759 The Jesuits are banished from Brazil.

1763 Rio de Janeiro *(above)* becomes the capital of Brazil.

1789 An independence plot led by Joaquim José da Silva Xavier, nicknamed *Tiradentes*—"the toothpuller"—is liquidated by the authorities.

1805 The sculptor Antônio Francisco Lisbôa, called O Aleijadinho, completes his masterwork—a series of statues for the Sanctuary of Bom Jesus near Ouro Prêto.

1808 To escape Napoleon's invasion of Portugal, the Portuguese Prince Regent, João, transfers his court to the Brazilian capital of Rio de Janeiro.

1816 The Prince Regent succeeds to the Portuguese throne as João VI.

1821 King João is recalled to Portugal to deal with the revolutionary ferment left by the Napoleonic Wars. His son, Dom Pedro, remains as regent of Brazil.

1822 Provoked by reactionary attitudes in Portugal, Dom Pedro proclaims Brazil's independence, becoming Emperor.

1824 Brazil receives a constitution on the liberal United States pattern.

1831–1840 The abdication of Pedro I leads to a decade of disorder and civil war under a regency, ending with the accession of Pedro II, aged 14, as Emperor. His enlightenment and concern during a 49-year reign bring great social and cultural advance.

1845 Coffee *(below)*, introduced to Brazil in the 18th century, accounts for almost half the nation's export earnings.

1887 Heitor Villa-Lobos, Brazil's greatest composer, is born in Rio.

1888 Slavery is abolished and some 700,000 slaves are freed.

1889 A military plot, fuelled by growing republican sentiment, secures Pedro's abdication and the end of the monarchy. A provisional regime adopts a presidential republican constitution in 1891.

1893 Opposition to dictatorial rule by military presidents leads to unrest and, in 1894, the election of Brazil's first civilian president.

1896 The Manaus Opera House, symbol of the short-lived Amazonian rubber boom, is opened. World demand for rubber was started by the invention of the vulcanizing process in 1839.

SEMANA·DE·ARTE· MODERNA ~ CATALOGO

1913 The Brazilian rubber boom suddenly dies as a result of competition from the Far East.

1917 Brazil enters World War I in support of the Allies.

1917 Pelo Telefone, the first samba ever recorded, becomes a popular hit.

1922 A Week of Modern Art *(catalogue above)* in São Paulo acts as a trigger for a sustained outburst of intense literary and artistic activity.

1929 Worldwide economic depression damages the Brazilian economy when coffee prices collapse.

1930 Gathering social and political unrest leads to a revolt headed by young military officers. Getúlio Vargas, Governor of the state of Rio Grande do Sul, comes to power.

1937 Getúlio Vargas *(right)* seizes absolute power.

1942 Brazil enters World War II on the side of the Allies.

1945 In a bloodless coup, a group of army officers force Vargas to resign. The following year, Brazil reverts to a democratic constitution.

1950 Vargas is re-elected as President. His term of office is marked by economic difficulties.

1954 His administration rocked by scandals, Vargas is forced to resign. He commits suicide on the same day.

1956 Juscelino Kubitschek, elected President in 1955, takes office and promises "fifty years of progress in five years".

1960 The new city of Brasília is declared the capital of Brazil.

1964 After the controversial legislation of a left-wing government has alienated conservative and military groups, a military coup establishes a dictatorship.

1973 Brazil's economic progress is crowned by the achievement of the world's fastest rate of economic growth for the year: 14 per cent.

1980 The overheated Brazilian economy crashes, leaving Brazil the world's greatest debtor nation.

1984 The Itaipu Dam, the world's largest, opens near the Brazilian border with Paraguay.

1985 Brazil returns to civilian government.

fortune in a city with a population which had grown to more than a million. Nobody knew it at the time, but the whole edifice of their prosperity was already beginning to crumble. Many years earlier, in 1876, the English botanist Henry Wickham had collected rubber seeds in the Amazon, which he had successfully propagated in London's Kew Gardens. The young trees grown from the seeds were then transferred to British plantations in the Far East, where they matured and were ready for tapping.

In 1913, the price of rubber fell to less than a quarter of the record price it had fetched in 1910. The following year the Far Eastern plantations put 72,546 tonnes of rubber on the market, and the price slumped still further. Many great Amazonian families went bankrupt immediately, and mass emigration southwards began. All along the great river, buildings stood empty and abandoned; cattle were penned in former drawing rooms among the rotting grand pianos and rusting harps; in Manaus the street lights went out because the municipality could no longer afford the electricity bills. The bonanza was over.

In these depressing economic circumstances, the outbreak of World War I was timely, bringing as it did an increased demand for Brazilian coffee, rubber and sugar. Brazil remained neutral until October 26, 1917; then, following German attacks on its shipping, it supported the Allies with naval units and considerable supplies of food and raw materials. During the war years, the volume of industrial production doubled, and by 1923 it had trebled. In turn, industrialization brought about greatly increased urbanization in cities such as São Paulo,

and encouraged the rise of a new industrial proletariat and middle class.

New skills and trades were brought to the cities by immigrant workers from Europe, who had started arriving in Brazil in the days of the late empire. The Japanese started arriving from 1908, swelling the influx, and before the outbreak of World War I annual immigration had reached record levels—half a million newcomers between 1911 and 1913. The new arrivals, mainly from Italy, Portugal and, to a lesser extent, from Spain, Germany, Poland and the Levant, continued to flow into Brazil until the 1930s, by which time some five million people born outside the country were estimated to have entered. Although the immigrant population never exceeded more than 6 per cent of the Brazilian-born population, the energy and new ideas they brought with them made a disproportionate impact on the economy and lifestyle of the country of their adoption, which remained for the most part a poor, rural and illiterate nation.

Even in the 1920s, 70 per cent of Brazilians worked on the land—land which was owned and largely governed by a privileged oligarchy whose wealth was now founded on coffee. But there was a new mood about, a passionate nationalist pride emerging in a new generation of idealistic intellectuals, civilians and soldiers alike, who repudiated the past and championed the forces for reform and change.

Young military officers—the *tenentes*, "lieutenants"—formed the most vociferous and effective opposition group. Without any ambition for personal power, they saw themselves as the guardians of the constitution. They wanted the establishment of a broadly based electorate, social legislation, ag-

rarian reform, nationalization of the mines, recognition for trade unions, and free primary and technical education throughout the country; they also wanted an end to the power monopoly of the coffee oligarchy, as well as an end to corruption, fraud, injustice, censorship and repression by government. Not least they wanted a strong central government for a united Brazil and an end to the growing separatist tendency of the regional states.

The officers struck their first blow after the 1922 presidential elections. In Rio, a small group of them staged a revolt at the military fort on Copacabana Beach. When they came under bombardment from military units loyal to the government, 18 of them—known as the "Copacabana 18"—made a last stand on the beach and were gunned down almost to a man. Although the rebellion ended in disaster, it initiated a series of army revolts which were to lead to the overthrow of the republic in 1930. By then the world was in recession. Coffee prices were plummeting, Brazilian exports had shrivelled and the exchange rate was at a record low. São Paulo, as the leading coffee state, was the worst affected region, and this meant that its coffee oligarchy was more vulnerable to attack.

The attack came when the powerful states of Minas Gerais and Rio Grande do Sul aligned themselves with the rebellious military element and other disaffected groups in a coalition they called the Liberal Alliance. Their nominee for President was the stocky, dynamic Governor of the southern state of Rio Grande do Sul, Getúlio Vargas, who stood for modernization and reform. When Vargas lost the election, the military revolted. An army junta seized control of the government, and insurrectionary troops marched towards the capital from the north and the south, unseating the State Governors one by one. Vargas, meanwhile, journeyed to Rio in triumph, enthusiastically acclaimed by all those who saw in him a symbol of revolutionary change, and in November 1930 the junta proclaimed Vargas President. Thus the old republic ended as it had begun—as the consequence of military intervention.

Getúlio Vargas was 47 years old when he assumed power in Brazil, and 71 when he finally relinquished it by the expediency of putting a bullet through his heart. His rule—first as constitutional President elected by Congress,

then as dictator appointed by himself, and finally as constitutional President chosen by the people—lasted nearly a quarter of a century, with an intermission of five years after World War II. Although his reputation was hotly disputed, his legacy to Brazil was undoubtedly tremendous.

At first Vargas made positive concessions to the *tenentes* who had helped him to power. But the honeymoon with radical elements of the army was short-lived. In 1932, insurgents in the state of São Paulo, convinced that Vargas was setting up a military dictatorship, rose up against him and were crushed. A new "strong man" had emerged in Brazil, just as other "strong men" were emerging in the totalitarian states of

Europe. Two years later, a new constitution was promulgated; it gave the central government greater powers over the regional states and incorporated many of the democratic demands of the revolutionaries, including the secret ballot, the representation of all classes in Congress, and female suffrage. Vargas also established trade unionism in the factories, brought them under state control, and imposed a minimum wage and maximum working week. Child labour was outlawed and women were given the same wage rights as men. These were the first measures ever taken to close the immense gap between rich and poor in Brazil, and they naturally won him huge support among the masses. But

OUTLAWS OF THE BRAZILIAN BACKLANDS

The bandit leader poses for a 1926 portrait.

In their finery, Lampião's gang pose with two of their camp followers.

Vargas was no democrat. In November 1937, while the country was preparing for presidential elections, he staged a coup, surrounded the two houses of Congress with troops, and put into effect a new constitution giving him virtually absolute powers.

The new regime, known as the *Estado Novo*, or New State, bore certain similarities to Mussolini's corporative state in Fascist Italy and Salazar's *Estado Novo* in Portugal. Vargas announced that 20th-century democracy was decadent and defunct. "The *Estado Novo*", he declared, "does not recognize the rights of the individual against the collective. Individuals do not have rights; they have duties. Rights belong to the collective!" So much power was now concentrated in Vargas' hands that he was able to

suppress all manifestations of democracy and the popular will. Political parties were banned, newspapers were censored, opponents were imprisoned.

Critics of Vargas' regime called it "Fascism with sugar", but his dictatorship did not descend to the worst barbarities of European counterparts. There were no concentration camps and no mass murders, and most political prisoners were soon released and allowed to go into exile. Nor was there any great confusion in Vargas' mind as to where his sympathies lay when World War II began. Loyal to the concept of Pan-Americanism, he followed the United States line. After the Japanese attack on Pearl Harbor, he opened Brazilian ports and airfields to the U.S. armed forces; and in August 1942, after several Brazilian merchant

ships had been torpedoed by German U-boats in the South Atlantic, he declared war on the Axis powers, a decision greeted with popular rejoicing.

Most notably in the war, the Brazilian navy took responsibility for all patrol duties in the South Atlantic, so allowing U.S. warships to be concentrated in the Far East; and in July 1944, a Brazilian expeditionary force of 25,000 men joined the 5th U.S. Army in Italy, where it distinguished itself in several battles, especially that of Monte Castello, and suffered nearly 2,500 casualties. One year later the troops returned to a heroes' welcome. The war had put Brazil in the leading place in the South American community and ensured her a place of honour in the United Nations. It had given a massive boost to Brazilian agriculture,

Of the many bandits who preyed on the backlands of north-eastern Brazil, the most notorious was Lampião, "the Lantern", who terrorized six states in the 1920s and 30s. Leading a large company of outlaws, he attacked individuals, ranches, even entire towns. Although his crimes included rape, arson, robbery, torture and murder, Lampião's occasional humane gestures—returning a robbery victim's wedding ring or giving to the poor—earned him the reputation of a Robin Hood. His exploits were glamorized in poems, books, films and an early documentary in which he himself starred.

After 16 years of skilfully evading capture, Lampião was shot by government troops in 1938. His severed head, publicly exhibited as proof of his death, was an attraction in a Salvador museum until 1969.

mining of minerals needed as war materials, and manufacturing industries. It had introduced army officers to American know-how and technology. And, indirectly, it had destroyed Vargas' political credibility.

Towards the end of the war, a group of prominent citizens in Minas Gerais had declared: "If we fight against Fascism at the side of the United States so that liberty and democracy may be restored to all people, certainly we are not asking too much in demanding for ourselves such rights and guarantees." The army concurred and put pressure on Vargas to set a date for free elections and a return to democracy. In October 1945, when it appeared that Vargas was planning to mobilize popular support and remain in power in perpetuity, a group of high-ranking officers ordered him to resign. Thus, the *Estado Novo*, like the empire and the republic before it, was ended by the intervention of the self-appointed guardian of public morality, the military.

Yet many Brazilians mourned the downfall of Vargas, for his regime had pioneered social legislation which had helped to alleviate the lot of the urban proletariat and had given them a sense of national identity for the first time in their history. It had reformed the educational system, diversified agriculture and, by the establishment of the steel mills at Volta Redonda and industrial development elsewhere, it had laid the foundation of a more sound economy for the future.

Such a record of achievement was sufficient to ensure that Vargas did not disappear completely from the political arena. He staged his comeback in 1950, following five years of honest and relatively liberal government under the presidency of General Eurico Gaspar Dutra. As leader of a new political front, the Brazilian Labour Party, Vargas successfully pitched his presidential election campaign at the working class and the rural landowners, and in January 1951 he was once again installed in the presidential palace in Rio. This time, it seemed, there could be no return to his pre-1945 style of government, and certainly, until 1953, Vargas attempted to abide by the new democratic constitution drawn up in 1946. But members of his administration were profoundly corrupt, and eventually they aroused the wrath of the military.

The crisis came in 1954 when the Brazilian journalist, Carlos Lacerda, attempted to expose the most blatant examples of government graft. In an attempt to assassinate Lacerda, Vargas' bodyguard shot Lacerda's bodyguard, who was an air force major. The political murder put the entire nation in an uproar, which was all the more intense because of rumours that Vargas was plotting to seize power on a more permanent basis. A delegation of senior army officers demanded the President's resignation.

It was the early dawn of August 24, when Vargas, who was still in his pyjamas, agreed to the officers' demands. He then retired to his bedroom to pen an open letter to the Brazilian people: "I can give nothing further but my blood. I choose this way to be always with you. I gave you my life. Now I offer my death. Serenely I take the first step on the road to eternity and leave my life to enter history." Some people claim that this letter is the work of another hand, but there seems no doubt that it was Vargas' own finger on the trigger of the pistol that buried a bullet in his heart.

After a short period of interim government, Juscelino Kubitschek, a former Governor of the state of Minas Gerais, whom many regarded as Vargas' political heir, came to power in January 1956. Kubitschek was a man of great personal charisma, restless energy and driving ambition, and he was determined to catapult his country to the forefront of the world's nations in the shortest possible time. "Fifty years' progress in five!" was his political slogan, and rapidly the industrialization of Brazil was thrown into top gear. Huge dams were constructed to help meet the increased demand for electrical power; the automobile industry was started up, and iron ore exports were doubled: it was a model of industrial growth built on an alliance of state planning and foreign and private

2

capital. Then, on a bleak, almost treeless wilderness on the central plateau of Brazil, Kubitschek gave the order for work to begin on the creation of the Brazilian dream—the building of the new capital of Brasília. This formidable undertaking was to serve a dual purpose for Kubitschek: it would mark a major step in Brazil's historic march into the interior, and it would ensure for himself an immortal niche in the country's history.

Responsibility for the design of all government buildings in the new capital fell on Kubitschek's personal friend, Brazilian architect, Oscar Niemeyer. The 100,000 workers who were brought into the wild and desolate location in the state of Goías worked round the clock to complete the project within the five-year term of the Kubitschek presidency. Since there was no railway, and only dirt roads which were subject to seasonal flooding, all the raw materials, including cement, were airlifted into the construction site at astronomical cost. It was typical of the way in which the ebullient—and visionary—Kubitschek shrugged aside the tremendous practical and financial obstacles that threatened this herculean labour.

In April 1960, amid rapturous official celebration, the new capital was formally inaugurated. It had cost £600 million and it was still not finished. Indeed, many members of the federal bureaucracy could find nowhere to live in Brasília, and some senior civil servants made the 2,800-kilometre round trip between the old capital and the new capital every working day. Brasília, it seemed, had brought the nation to the brink of bankruptcy, and inflation now began to spiral towards giddy heights in an economy superheated by over-rapid industrial expansion. Moreover, government corruption and waste had not diminished. In the south of the country, political and economic power remained in the hands of a tiny minority; in the north, the people were still abysmally poor.

In January 1961, when Kubitschek stepped down from the presidency, he left behind him a nation in a state of financial chaos. His critics said that instead of "50 years' progress in five", he had achieved "40 years' inflation in four". Kubitschek's two presidential successors, Jânio Quadros and João Goulart, were destined to founder on Brazil's economic rocks, and neither served a full five-year term of office. The same economic forces contributed to the chaos that occasioned the army generals' coup of 1964 and, 21 years later, to the restoration of democracy by a military government whose illusions of economic grandeur had rebounded on them.

But Kubitschek's historic legacy remained Brasília—as modernistic as a space city but as inconvenient as a frontier town, a pioneer's dream and a pedestrian's nightmare—stood foursquare under the skies of the great central plateau. Shaped like a bird or an aeroplane—some would say, like a drawn bow aimed into the interior— Brasília was the symbol of a new future and a nation reborn.

Whatever troubles still lay ahead in the 1960s, Brasília provided the irresistible impulse that would open up the sparsely inhabited and underdeveloped wilderness of the interior and unite its disjointed parts, so that one day the Brazilian nation would be able to fulfil its promise as *opaís do futuro*— the land of the future.

Standing on a newly cleared tract of land in 1957, surveyors lay out the site plan of Brasília, which three years later was inaugurated as the new capital of Brazil. As well as government offices, houses and a commercial centre, the project included a 30-kilometre-long artificial lake and a yacht club.

3

Two jubilant young Brazilians wave their national flag during the election campaign of 1985. The central slogan "Order and Progress" is emblazoned across a map of the night sky as seen from Rio: the constellation of 23 stars represents the states of the federal republic and the unity of the people.

RICH AND POOR, BLACK AND WHITE

In his seminal work *The Masters and the Slaves*, the Brazilian sociologist Gilberto Freyre documented the crucial role of plantation society in the development of Brazilian civilization. "Like a powerful god," he concluded, it "divided us into enslaver and enslaved." In 1934, when Freyre's book was published, slavery had been abolished in Brazil for nearly half a century but its heritage was still apparent everywhere. A network of wealthy landowners continued to wield immense power and the black ex-slaves, for the most part, remained firmly at the bottom of a steep social ladder.

Since the 1930s, and especially in the past two decades, industrialization, urbanization and massive population growth have profoundly altered the shape of this society. Seventy per cent of Brazilians now live in cities. The masters of old have been swamped by a burgeoning middle class, which today numbers some 30 million. A manufacturing working class has come into being. Yet still discernible within the new outlines of the country's class structure are the quintessentially Brazilian features that Freyre pinpointed. Disparities in wealth and position are still enormous. Those of good family gain disproportionate influence through their assiduously cultivated connections. And most blacks are still found among the poor.

At the pinnacle of the social scale, the descendants of the slave-owning aristocrats live on in their spacious colonial houses on the coffee and sugar plantations. Often their lifestyle is quite simple; even in the colonial era, enormous fortunes were rarely made in Brazil, and such wealth as a family once possessed may well have been dissipated. But the country landowners wield power, especially in the north and north-east. Their tenants, and the tradespeople who depend on them, defer to their political views and vote according to their direction.

Often the landowners own local newspapers, and thus mould the opinions of a wider circle of country people than those with whom they have direct dealings. The landowners frequently have a hand in appointments in the police force and the judiciary. They maximize their impact on regional politics through complex webs of family connections.

In Brazil's colonial days, the *parentela*—or extended family—came to embrace not just blood relations but also in-laws, adopted children and godchildren. The patriarch of a family would use the *parentela* to consolidate his interests, marrying his daughters to wealthy neighbours, securing powerful godfathers for his sons. Once recruited thus into his sphere, they could be expected to act in his interests. These days, Brazilian girls—even those from traditionally minded families—expect to make up their own minds about whom they will marry. But family con-

In downtown São Paulo, a group of young boys sleep huddled together on the pavement, protected by plastic bags and a thin blanket. They are part of the growing army of a million children in the city who live rough all year round, abandoned by parents who cannot afford to support them.

tinues to command powerful loyalties among the rural aristocracy.

To be a member of the urban Establishment—the band of powerful businessmen, civil servants and professionals who make up perhaps 5 per cent of the population—family connections are not always crucial nowadays. Taking advantage of the opportunities provided by the economic miracle, a few talented men have climbed to the top without benefit of family. Most of the newcomers are the ambitious and hard-working descendants of fairly recent immigrants—the Italians, Japanese, Czechs and others who arrived in the early years of this century looking for opportunites in a land of potential.

But the majority among the wealthy and powerful are not first-generation success stories. They come from families comfortably established for several decades.

The urban élite sets great store by education. Virtually every child is expected to aim for university. From the late 1960s, Brazil's university system—consisting of both state-funded and private colleges—expanded hugely. In the course of the 1970s, the number of undergraduate places grew from less than half a million to more than a million, and the graduate places grew from 3,000 to 38,000. Many young adults study abroad for a few years after taking a first degree at a

Brazilian university. They arrive home with masters' degrees and doctorates from famous European and North American places of learning and glide smoothly into high-powered jobs in industry, government or the professions.

Qualifications, however, are not their only weapons in the struggle for success. Anyone who has strings to pull exploits them to a far greater extent than is normal in the United States and Europe. When somebody lands a plum job, a natural question for his friends to ask is: "Who put you up for it?" Very often the answer is an uncle or a godfather—evidence that the *parentela* is still integral to the functioning of urban Brazil. Many among the new breed of superbly educated Brazilians, meritocrats on the surface, turn out on close acquaintance to have a connection with one of the country's old lineages. Family means a great deal to such people. The history and traditions of their line are compelling topics of conversation. They maintain regular contact with tribes of distant cousins and in-laws. For some, attending baptisms, weddings, confirmation services and other family events can occupy so much time that outside contacts are difficult to maintain.

Professional salaries are very uneven in Brazil. A top civil servant whose uncle is a minister will earn a large salary. An ordinary administrator will be badly paid. A fashionable doctor can easily earn five times as much as one with a modest practice in an undistinguished part of town. But salaries at the top in Brazil are high by any standard, and the upper middle class live better than their counterparts in most other countries. Many have a house on an estate in the country as well as a smart apartment in town. They belong to clubs where they can play tennis or golf, swim or eat in exclusive company, often with their membership fee paid by their employers. They relax at away-from-it-all beach resorts and travel widely as tourists within Brazil. They often spend their Saturdays shopping in huge multi-storey malls built on American lines.

At a more intimate level, lifestyles are equally Western. For all their concern with the ramifications of kin, the Brazilian élite live as nuclear families in their city apartments. The women usually marry young, the men rather later. Divorce was only legalized in 1977 but already carries little stigma, nor is there overwhelming social pressure to remarry: for second and subsequent unions, couples often just live together. Portuguese has the same word for "wife" and "woman", so at social gatherings it is easy to gloss over the legal status of a relationship. Many of the Brazilians engaged in the hectic search for fulfilling relationships are as addicted to psychoanalysis as New Yorkers and Californians.

But the lifestyle of the Brazilian élite is not altogether like that of the equivalent class in North America or Europe. The most striking difference is, perhaps, the availability of servants in Brazil. Domestics figure large as status symbols, and a great deal of social gossip consists of minute assessments of the merits and failings of staff. The average well-to-do family has two female servants—usually black—one of whom lives in. Even the lower middle class—shop-owners, clerical workers and the like—normally have a maid.

One third of the women employed in Brazil are in domestic service, acting as nannies, cooks and cleaning maids. Those who live in are given a small bedroom close to the kitchen. Although they are allowed a siesta in the afternoon, they have little time they can call entirely their own. They are often paid less than the meagre legal minimum wage—in theory the amount necessary to keep a family of four, although in practice it falls considerably short of that. However, like the house slaves of the early plantation days, the domestics very often have a close relationship with the families they serve and, in particular, play an important role in the upbringing of their employers' children.

Thanks to the ubiquitous servants, upper-middle-class Brazilian women never have to concern themselves with chores such as cooking or cleaning. Many live a life of leisure and self-indulgence. They spend their time tanning themselves on the beach, paying daily visits to the hairdresser and shopping in smart boutiques.

In marked contrast to this pampered breed are Brazil's professional women, some of whom hold key positions in commerce, academia and the law. Like their brothers, they are formidably well educated, often at foreign universities. When they step into senior jobs, they are effective and highly regarded. Many of them support Brazil's well-organized feminist movement.

Feminism came late to Brazil. In colonial days, women's only roles were those of wife and mother, and they led lives of almost monastic seclusion. Their status did begin to change in this century when the development of new service industries provided a springboard for women to enter the labour market. In 1907, girls of "good social condition" were admitted as telephonists in Rio de Janeiro and, in 1917, the first women were allowed to join the civil service. In 1934, women were granted the vote. But Brazil was only a fringe combatant in World War II and women therefore missed the impetus the war gave their sex elsewhere for a re-evaluation of their capabilities. It was not until the 1970s that women became more independent, thanks to the job opportunities that were created by economic growth, and the spreading use of contraception.

In São Paulo and other major cities, modern Western feminism began to make an impact at this time. International Women's Year in 1975 led to the setting up of the Centre for the Development of the Brazilian Woman, which began investigating women's

3

and children's health issues. At the same time there appeared many voluntary organizations concerning themselves with community problems such as sanitation, education and housing. Such campaigns cut across class barriers: working-class women, often encouraged by the Catholic Church, gained confidence through their participation in local pressure groups.

It was in spite of the opposition of the Catholic Church, however, that General Ernesto Geisel, a Lutheran who was President of Brazil from 1974 to 1979, gave official support to family

planning programmes in the cities. For both religious and nationalistic reasons, the country had been very reluctant to do anything to discourage population growth, but when President Geisel's Catholic successor, President Figueiredo, spoke about the need for "responsible parenthood", the message for women was clear. The 1980 census showed that the birth rate had dropped markedly.

Despite the new-found confidence of women, old attitudes as to the roles of men and women are dying hard. Many Brazilian men have trouble in taking

the new professional women seriously. One manifestation of the old attitude to women is the inordinate importance placed on their appearance at work. Advertisements for female staff specify good looks and youth as essentials. The majority of Brazilian women, far from resenting the requirement as sexist, cheerfully play the game. They arrive for job interviews dressed to kill and use their femininity as a weapon in office politics. However, their insouciance turns to panic around the age of 35, and the enormous emphasis on youth makes them terrified of the first wrinkle. Brazil has a plastic surgery industry to rival Florida's.

Another area where feminism and traditional values combine uneasily is the issue of domestic servants. Many feminists feel it wrong in principle to keep other women in such a dependent situation and to pay them so little. Some feel so embarrassed about their exploitative position that, when circles of feminists meet in private apartments, they take care not to raise the issue of domestics until the servant has retired to her room. But in practice the development of such women's careers is underpinned by the existence of maids and childminders; they would have difficulty in managing on their own, and few of them try. Other feminists salve their conscience by telling themselves that, despite all the injustices of the situation, poor women want the jobs and it is therefore their duty to provide employment.

Meanwhile, feminist ideas are beginning to filter through to the maid-servants themselves. In the big cities, domestic servants are beginning to associate in small groups in order to press for such improvements as the government minimum wage, a day off a week and the right to unionize.

Domestic servants make up just a fraction of the great mass of Brazilians who endure poverty. The middle class, though large numerically, accounts for less than a quarter of the population. Ninety million Brazilians live in conditions ranging from basic but cheerful to those of appalling destitution.

Some of the worst deprivation is experienced in the backlands. In the north-east, the masses scratch a precarious subsistence from small family patches of parched earth with a few

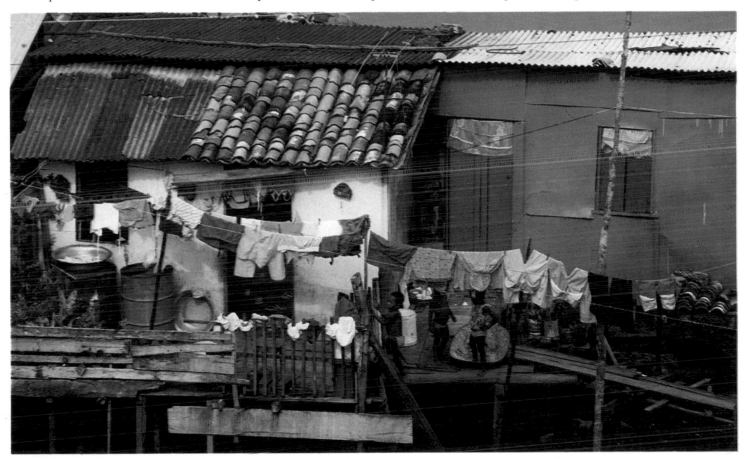

Favela houses cling to the steep granite hillsides of Rio de Janeiro *(opposite)* and perch on stilts in the mud flats of Salvador *(above)*. Some are solidly built, boasting power lines and television aerials, but their foundations are precarious: landslides and floods can cause widespread devastation.

maize plants and perhaps half a dozen chickens. The people are lucky if they eat meat three times a year. Although there are mining and petrochemical projects in the region, these involve only a tiny number of skilled workers. The majority still depend for their cash income on casual labour in the plantations at pitiful wages. They are heavily dependent on the plantation owners for patronage, and for assistance if they run into trouble with the law. They live in huts built from whatever materials they can scrape together. The 1980 census showed that only 17 per cent of homes in the northeast had electric light, compared with two thirds in the south-east; only one in 10 homes was connected to mains drainage, compared with seven out of 10 in the south-east; and only one in five had running water, compared with more than half in the south-east.

It is not surprising that the rural poor have been flocking to the cities in search of a better life. The move to the cities began as early as the 1930s and later accelerated sharply with the rapid industrial growth of the 1960s

and 1970s. Brazilians, like so many others, see the cities as places of hope: they crave the bright lights, the chance of a quick *cruzeiro*. They like the noise and activity—*movimento*, as they call it admiringly.

For millions, the move from the countryside brought its rewards. The miracle decade of the 1970s brought upward mobility to almost everybody who found employment. The proportion of the work force who earned the minimum wage or less dropped from almost two thirds to just over a third.

The gains must be seen in perspective. Although the élite of the new working class—employees in the car factories of São Paulo, for example—earn between twice and five times the minimum wage, international car manufacturers still find them cheap to employ. More than 60 per cent of the working population still earns less than twice the minimum wage—which, by developed nations' standards, means they are poor. What is more, recession in the 1980s has thrown many out of work, besides slowing progress for nearly all the others. And many have

merely exchanged rural for urban misery, without bettering themselves at all. To those for whom the bright lights of the cities have proved a mirage, there is nowhere else to go, no hope.

The history of two of the new city dwellers, Luís and Teotista, illustrates the possibilities and pitfalls that open up for the country folk prepared to try their luck in the cities. Luís and Teotista used to be neighbours in the north-eastern state of Pernambuco, which is often affected by years of severe drought. In 1970 they decided to leave their families in the village and join the exodus to São Paulo, in search of jobs and a better life.

With 50 others, they made the long trek south on the back of a truck, hanging on to the *pau de arara*—the "parrot's perch" formed by two poles running alongside. The first few days were rough going, over dirt tracks, but then they travelled on paved roads and after two weeks they entered the big city. Luís went to stay with a brother in São Bernardo, the motor manufacturing suburb; Teotista, who had no relatives to help, looked for work on a building site. Over the next 15 years, their lives diverged sharply.

Luís' brother found him a job in the car factory, where he became a skilled toolmaker, and a couple of years after he arrived he sent money north for his wife Bernadette and his two young children to join him. They now have a third child and Bernadette works at the local kindergarten school. The two eldest children are both doing well: the eldest, Teresa, hopes to become a teacher, the second, Airton, wants to be an engineer.

The family live in São Bernardo, in their own house which Luís, like most working-class Brazilians, designed and built himself with the help of relatives and friends. Whenever there is cash for more materials, he adds an extra room or pushes out a wall. Luís has been laid off work occasionally, but never for more than a month or two, and the family have always managed to get by. They have a colour television and own a second-hand car—a Volkswagen Beetle—and on Sundays they sometimes drive to the beach or go fishing. The miracle has brought suc-

cess for Luís and his family, and they are firmly on the ladder upwards.

But fortune did not smile on Teotista, who has never progressed beyond being an unskilled labourer and has twice been injured at work on building sites, where nobody bothers with such things as safety helmets or boots. His wife Eva and six children migrated from the north-east to join him; four more children were born after Eva arrived. The family live way out of town in a tiny tumbledown shack, built from old lengths of wood and flattened oil drums, the gaps plastered with mud and a sheet of plastic held down with bricks for a roof. A filthy stream serves as a sewer.

When he has a job, it costs Teotista a quarter of his daily wage just to travel to and from work in a jam-packed bus. These days, with civil construction at a much lower level than in the 1970s, he is often out of work. He drinks a lot, and sometimes disappears for days on end. Eva has to struggle to bring up their children on what she can earn as a cleaning woman. The children are often ill: one caught infantile

paralysis in the north and his legs are both paralysed; another has twice been rushed to hospital with pneumonia. All are undernourished, below average size and backward. The eldest girl, Sandra, has become a prostitute, while Maurício, one of the eldest boys, has been tempted into petty crime, picking pockets in the city centre.

Teotista and Eva once tried going back to the north, but life was even worse there, with no land to cultivate. They heard through the grapevine about Luís' good fortune and, still with a tiny seed of hope in their hearts, returned to São Paulo to start again.

The endurance of such families seems almost heroic, and Teotista's story is by no means unusual in Brazil. The mass of the people can apparently be pushed and asked to make sacrifices to a degree almost unthinkable in other countries without provoking an explosion. This is largely because during the boom years of the 1970s the pace of change and the degree of material progress enjoyed by most Brazilians was so great and so concentrated that the majority still feel dazed by it. Even those who missed out have a relative or acquaintance who prospered. People who are not utterly ground down by misfortune continue to believe that if they keep trying, work hard and encourage their children to study, they will get a good job and their family will make progress.

Unfortunately, the better education of which Brazilians dream is rarely available. During the 1960s and 1970s, while it was pouring resources into the university system that benefited a small fraction of the population, Brazil neglected its primary schools. Poor pay

for teachers meant low professional standards. The inadequate teachers still fill the primary education system, and the quality of instruction is extremely low. Pupils often fail to reach the standard required at the end of the school year and are required to repeat a grade. Less than two thirds of those who complete the first grade go beyond the fourth grade, and less than a quarter of the same group goes on to secondary education. Recently, the imbalance in the allocation of educational resources has been recognized, and much attention is focused on the plight

of the primary schools. But it will be a number of years before the faults in the system can be remedied.

Even in those pockets where the schools are good—Brasília has a better reputation than most other cities—educational attainments are not high because many children drop out of school to earn money. In families such as Teotista's, they become invaluable breadwinners at a tender age. A boy or girl may become a domestic servant or office messenger, may load shoppers' bags in the supermarkets, or try to sell something at road junctions when cars

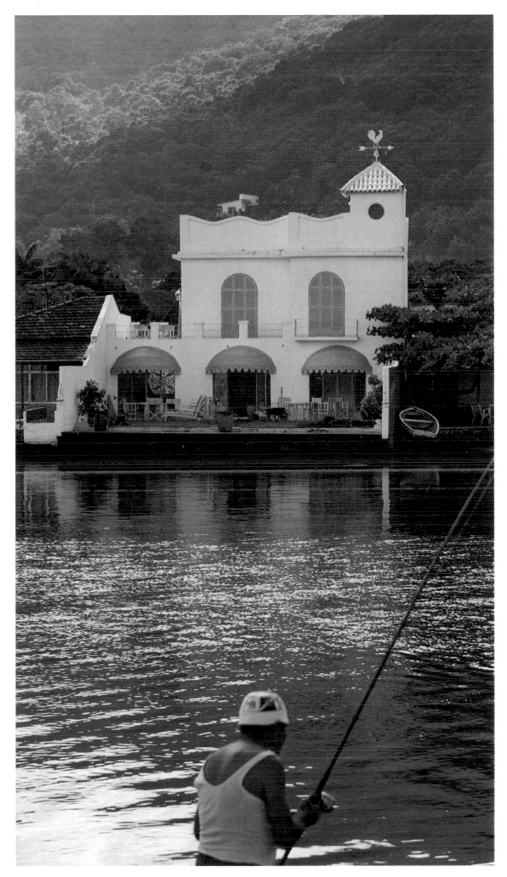

stop for traffic lights. When all these small sums are added up, there may be enough to feed and clothe the family, and perhaps buy a small plot of land on which to build a home.

When even this existence proves impossible, there may be no alternative to the shanty town or *favela*. São Paulo, Brazil's economic capital, had fewer than 40,000 shanty dwellers in 1970, but the 1980 census revealed a surge to nearly 400,000. By the mid-1980s, with a third of the work force unemployed, the figure had risen another 200,000.

A *favela* starts with an *invasão*, which is sometimes organized but is usually a spontaneous invasion by homeless families of unused land near the heart of a city. It may be swampy or, perhaps, the side of a hill that is too steep to be developed with conventional buildings. Thousands of people cram themselves into a jumble of shacks made from packing cases, old corrugated iron sheets and cardboard, often with one shanty leaning on the next for support. The stink that comes from the unpaved alleyways between the houses is appalling—in many places there are no sewers and the only way human waste and garbage are disposed of is by a heavy downpour of rain.

In some *favelas* there is no water supply, so the inhabitants carry water they have taken from public fountains or fire hydrants to their houses in kerosene tins. Inevitably, the explosive growth of *favelas* has brought a wave of disease and a worrying upswing in Brazil's infant mortality rate, which had dropped steadily since the 1940s. In 1980, 14 per cent of the children born in São Paulo died before they reached their first birthday.

The *favela* dwellers sometimes obtain an electricity supply illegally from

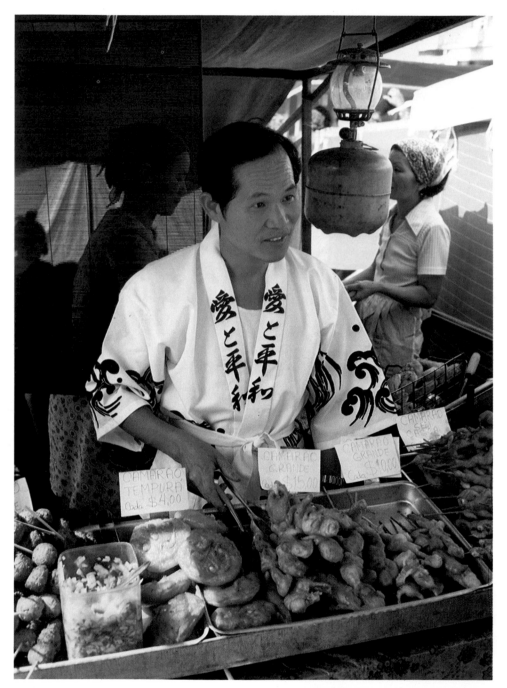

In the Japanese quarter of São Paulo, a stallholder offers *camarão grande*—**king prawns fried in batter. More than 300,000 Japanese emigrated to Brazil in the first half of this century, and most settled in São Paulo state, forming Japan's largest overseas community.**

the national grid, while others connect up to the supplies of neighbouring houses to whom they pay a handsome premium for the privilege. Post is often addressed to a nearby house with a permanent address, and redistributed from there by the *favela*'s own unofficial postal service.

Many *favelas* have been cleared by municipal authorities and their inhabitants moved to subsidized housing or flats on the outskirts of the city, but this solution is not popular because of the additional travelling expenses involved and a general dislike among Brazilians of being away from the city centres. In cases where the inhabitants of a *favela* begin to feel they are not in imminent danger of being dispossessed, or where they have managed to lease the land from its owner, they usually begin making improvements to their houses, which can end up reasonably comfortable. A strong sense of community usually develops. Small neighbourhood shops spring up selling goods on extended credit—though at inflated prices, since the shop-owners do not have access to wholesalers.

Many families, in keeping with their rural backgrounds, keep chickens and even pigs in their minuscule yards. Some set up tiny businesses, repairing cars or making gewgaws for sale. With no unemployment benefit to fall back on, the rest survive by roaming the streets in search of waste paper, bottles and scrap metal, by scouring the rubbish tips for food, and by begging.

Under the stresses of poverty and bad living conditions, many families disintegrate. The most tragic aspect of the breakdown is the plight of the children. Of an estimated 6.2 million children in the region of São Paulo, nearly one in five lives in the streets, not so much orphaned as abandoned by parents so racked with poverty that they can no longer support them. The main worry of the children is that they will be apprehended by the police and locked up in a FEBEM, the acronym of the Foundation for the Education and Benefit of Minors. Intended as asylums for abandoned children, FEBEM depots long ago gave up any attempt to live up to the intention of their title and have simply become desolate and vandalized institutions where a token percentage of the children can be kept off the streets for a few nights.

Many of the "sufferers of the street", as they are known, are addicted to glue sniffing as a comfort and to stifle pangs of hunger. Some support themselves by scavenging garbage for the collecting lorries; some eke a living as shoe cleaners or street traders, and some are hired by shopkeepers as assistant security staff at half the legal wage. Others lead a life that revolves round the gambling machine arcades, prostitution and petty thievery.

Crime has become a serious problem in urban Brazil. Thousands of murders are reported each year in São Paulo and Rio; many more go unreported. Around a quarter of all homes in the largest cities are burgled in any one year. Hold-ups have become almost commonplace on the bus route between Rio and São Paulo. Despite armed security guards protecting the banks, shops and apartment blocks, and heavy policing in the better parts of the cities, the middle class is extremely worried. High crime rates undoubtedly reflect the desperate straits of countless Brazilians; many of the urban gangsters are the abandoned children of yesterday.

Even a casual visitor to Brazil recognizes that the underprivileged portion of society contains a disproportionate number of dark-skinned people. Quantifying that impression is, however, fraught with difficulty, not less because of the Brazilian spectrum of skin shades, with every colour gradation represented. Since whites began inter-breeding with the native Indians four centuries ago, and with the Negro slaves not very long after, it is hardly surprising that the blending has been thorough. On the beaches, on the streets, the majority of Brazilians seem to be a mixed race, any permutation of European, African and, to a lesser extent, Amerindian.

The picture does vary somewhat from region to region. In the *favelas* of the large cities one could imagine one-self in West Africa. In the far south, the features of the 20th-century European immigrants predominate, while in the north and north-east, there are still numerous backlanders who have a pro-nouncedly Amerindian physiognomy. But millions of Brazilians everywhere fall into one of the intermediate categories generously provided for in Brazilian Portuguese. Between *côr do carvão*, "coal colour", (a dark Negroid type) and *moreno* (toast-coloured with straight or wavy hair) words can be found to distinguish more than a dozen different physiognomies.

At the time of Brazil's first census, taken in 1872, whites accounted for less than 40 per cent of the population. Over the next half-century, immi-gration from Europe, the Middle East and Japan considerably lightened the Brazilian people. The 1950 census, the last to seek racial origins, classified the population as 62 per cent white, 11 per cent black and 27 per cent mixed blood. The census can only be a rough guide since it required people to make their own judgement as to their colour. Most objective observers would assess the proportion of pure whites as con-siderably less than 62 per cent. But distinctions between white and near-white are of little consequence in Bra-

zil. The most important division comes somewhere in the middle of the mixed-blood or *mulato* group. The experience of the dark *mulatos* in Brazilian society is essentially the same as that of the blacks, while light *mulatos* can live similar lives to whites. The blacks, to-gether with the dark *mulatos*, make up around 30 per cent of the population.

Most Brazilians insist that the ex-perience of blacks and whites in their country only differs to the extent that the blacks are poorer. Brazilian ortho-doxy acknowledges that the historical handicap of slavery has placed most blacks in the lowest classes but it does not admit to any racial discrimination today. Brazilians proudly describe their nation as a racial democracy, where people of every shade have an equal chance of social advancement. Indeed, so convinced are they of the truth of their claim that any attempt to question it is met with incredulity and hurt pride.

The philosophy of many in Brazil is to encourage a process called *branque-amento*—literally, "whitening". The idea is that continued interbreeding between the races will eventually make it impossible to separate out those who have African origins. Immigration of whites, although on a very small scale nowadays, also contributes towards the whitening of the nation. For the individual black with ambitions, the Brazilians have a phrase: "money whitens". It is widely held that as a black becomes wealthier or better edu-cated, so his blackness counts for less. This Brazilians see as evidence that there is no prejudice against blacks as such, but merely against their low socio-economic position.

Several facts appear superficially to support the belief that blacks are equal

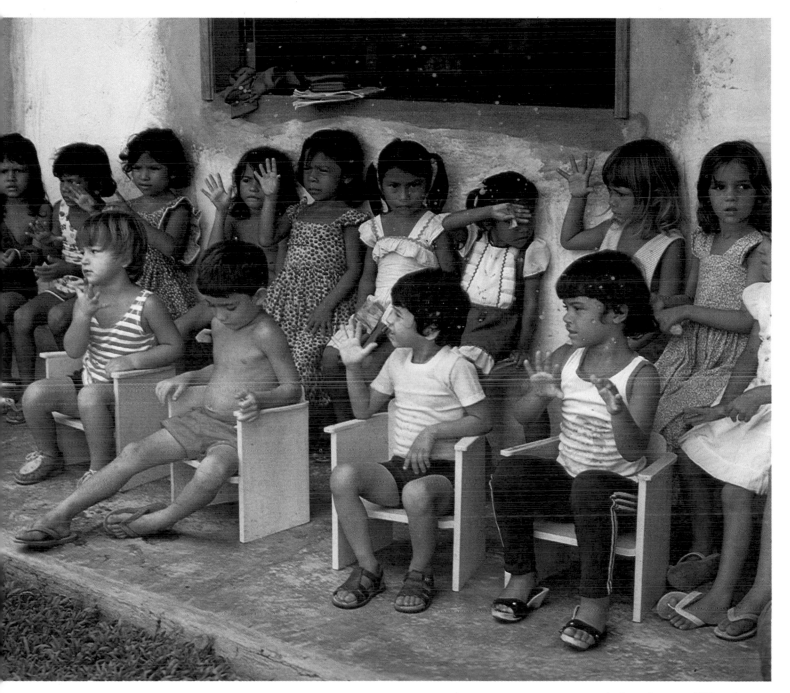

A class of young children learn to count on their fingers at a village school in Amazonia. Primary education is free in Brazil, and theoretically compulsory, but trained teachers are so scarce in country areas that only one in seven children completes elementary school.

3

in Brazil. First of all, there is the fact that overt racial discrimination has long been outlawed. The 1946 constitution prohibited discrimination on grounds of colour, and the ban was given legal teeth in 1951 with the passing of a law that specified penalties for race discrimination in public places. Then there are the crowds in the streets and on the beaches, where people of quite different hues mingle together and socialize happily. Case histories can be produced, moreover, to show that mixed blood has never been an absolute barrier to advancement. Recently, there have been the successes of Pelé, the black footballer, and numerous pop musicians; and as far back as 1909, there was even a President of mixed blood, Nilo Peçanha.

Certainly, the friendliness between the races in Brazil is unique in a country with a slave-owning history. Freyre, while documenting the crucial division in society that slave ownership produced, recorded many mitigating factors in colonial society. He stressed the affectionate relations between masters and slaves, and the lack of prejudice against the miscegenation of races. In his view, the Portuguese harboured considerable respect for the Africans, both on account of having once been ruled themselves by Moors and because of their Catholic religion, which obliged them to see the slaves not as mere chattels but as creatures with souls that could be saved.

Freyre's widely respected views have contributed in large measure to the myth of Brazil as a multiracial society free from the problems of racism that beset other countries. And there is much truth in that picture. The easy-going tolerance that dates back to the colonial period, together with the

legal framework of equality, has at least prevented the kind of bitter polarization of black and white that has occurred in other countries. Although the Indians have suffered deeply at the hands of those who came later, racial violence is otherwise unknown in Brazil. And, with no tangible grievance to unite them, Brazilian blacks have been slow to react against the subtler forms of discrimination that have persisted since the slave epoch.

In the 1950s, the blacks of Brazil could count themselves far better off than those of the southern states of the U.S., who were banned from public places and most institutions of higher education, and debarred from all but menial jobs. American blacks had to fight for their civil rights in the 1960s, and in doing so not only won political reforms but also changed the whole climate of society. No similar transformation of racial attitudes has taken place in Brazil. As a result, clear-sighted observers find evidence of both widespread racial prejudice in Brazil today and many pressures on blacks and dark *mulatos* to remain in a subservient position.

Jokes about the morals, intelligence, honesty and reliability of blacks are commonplace, for example, and black women are subtly denigrated. In Brazilian folklore, the *mulata* is passionate and promiscuous—the ideal mistress, but not suitable as a wife.

In employment, blacks often have extreme difficulty reaching high position. Until recently, black Brazilians, however suitably qualified, were not admitted to the diplomatic service or to the Brazilian navy, which considered itself the élite of the country's armed forces. There are still very few blacks at the upper levels of the admin-

istration, business and commerce; and a mere handful of the members of the 548-strong Brazilian Congress are black. The poverty of blacks cannot go all the way to explaining these low figures: the immigrants from Europe and Asia who have settled in Brazil over the past 100 years often possessed no more than the blacks during their early years, and have succeeded in rising rapidly. The much-vaunted people of mixed race who do reach the top are far more often pale-skinned *mulatos* than really black.

The job advertisements that appear in the press for shop assistants or clerical staff frequently specify *boa aparência*. Everyone in Brazil knows that that phrase can be translated as "white or pale-skinned" as well as its literal meaning of "good appearance". So blacks take the hint and do not apply.

The convention regarding *boa aparência* is typical of the situation in Brazil today. There is no overt act of discrimination, because there is no need for one. The system was neatly satirized recently by Millor Fernandes, a Rio cartoonist, with the epigram "there is no racism in Brazil: the blacks know their place".

The minority of blacks who do make progress up the social scale are generally reluctant to jeopardize their position by complaining about prejudice. Rather, they tend to understate their blackness, and many marry fairer-skinned people in order that their children will be paler. Nevertheless, Afro-Brazilian consciousness has been slowly emerging.

The first organization to stand up for the rights of black people was the Brazilian Negro Front, which was founded in São Paulo in 1931. Committed to non-violence, it created

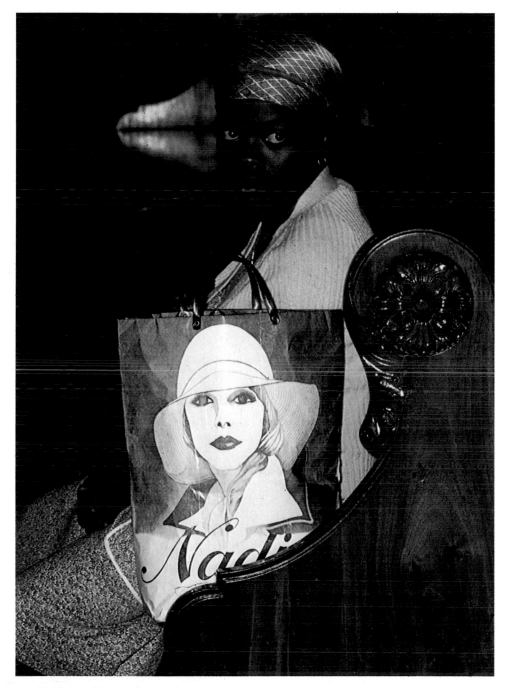

a political party, organized political demonstrations and published a newspaper. In 1937, during the Vargas dictatorship, it was banned, along with other political organizations.

There was a revival of black consciousness in 1945 under Abdias do Nascimento, a playwright who is considered the father of the modern black rights movements in Brazil. Nascimento founded the Afro-Brazilian Democratic Committee, which was anaesthetized in its turn after the military coup of 1964. Despite the inspiration of the decolonization of Africa and the progress of the civil rights movement in the United States, black political awareness in Brazil subsided into a long period of quiescence. It was not dead, however. As successive military governments relaxed their authoritarianism, a group called the Unified Black Movement against Racial Discrimination brought 5,000 people out into the streets of São Paulo in 1978 to protest against an overt act of racism in a sports club. It was the first public demonstration against racism seen in Brazil for many years, and it heralded a heightened racial consciousness.

Since Brazil's return to democracy in 1985, many new groups promoting Afro-Brazilian cultural identity and protesting against various forms of discrimination have appeared. Most of them are non-militant. It is still only a tiny handful of blacks who participate in such groups but their influence is spreading. The number of black Brazilians who are proud of their colour and prepared to insist on their rights is growing. Although Freyre's image of masters and slaves is still very relevant to the Brazilian social order, it may not be long before the slaves shake off their invisible shackles.

The black worshipper in a Rio church and the idealized Caucasian portrayed on her bag bear silent testimony to the social gulf between white and black in Brazil. Despite laws forbidding racial discrimination, most of the nation's estimated 12 million blacks remain at the poorest levels of society.

COWBOYS OF THE PAMPAS

Photographs by Claus C. Meyer

For 200 years, the vast pampas of southern Brazil have been the trackless domain of cattle, horses and *gaúchos*, the free-spirited cowboys who ride with the herds. Usually of mixed Portuguese and Indian ancestry, the first *gaúchos* were true nomads of the grasslands. They rode where they pleased, taming mustangs when they wanted fresh mounts. If they needed money, they killed the half-wild cows that roamed the pampas for their valuable hides, leaving the carcasses to rot in the sun.

Today, the cattle are branded, the pampas are fenced and the *gaúchos* are employees of ranchers and beef companies. Responsible for enormous herds of prized cattle, they ride for long days, driving animals from one gigantic pasture to another. They notch ears and brand haunches, dose sick cows, de-horn calves and castrate young bulls. Now, their independent spirits are tethered by their rigorous jobs. Yet their knowledge of the pampas, their stamina and their superb horsemanship have not changed since the 19th century, when poems and ballads enshrined them as Brazil's folk heroes.

On a round-up, several hundred head of cattle are herded through a gate between pastures. Shifting animals to fresh grazing or driving them to the slaughterhouse can mean a week on the trail, with the *gaúchos* sleeping at night under the stars, using their ponchos and saddles as beds.

Surrounded by *domadors*, the *gaúcho* horse-breakers, a wild-eyed colt rears in terror as he feels the weight of the saddle for the first time. Although this moment is often frenzied, the horses are broken in gradually, with gentle handling over many months. The traditional saddle, constructed without a pommel or cantle, is a sandwich of leather pads and woollen blankets. A thick sheepskin lies on top to prevent saddle soreness during long rides. The stirrups are a recent innovation: at one time *gaúchos* rode barefoot, gripping leather straps between their toes to keep their balance.

Gleaming with silver medallions and coins, a *gaúcho*'s wide leather belt is a treasured part of his outfit, often passed from father to son. It is buckled over a woven blue sash and a battered hide apron which protects the legs.

Clasped in fingers stained by the bloody work of gelding calves, a string of beads serves as a tally of cattle in the herd: each bead represents 50 animals. The beads hang from a belt which also holds a revolver—now a rarely-used reminder of more dangerous days on the pampas.

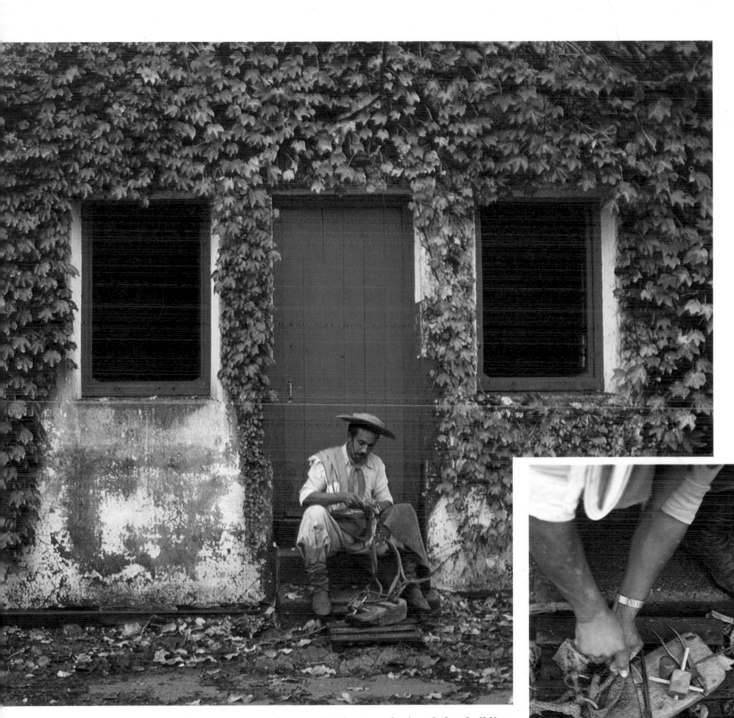

On the steps of a vine-clad outbuilding,
a *gaúcho* punches new holes in his
horse's bridle. The men are skilled
harness-makers, fashioning their own
tack *(right)* from the grasslands'
plentiful supply of cowhide.

On a rainy night the *gaúchos* move their usual outdoor barbecue into the stable, where accordion music rises above the sizzle of roasting meat. The menu is

always the same: bitter herbal tea sipped from a gourd, and prime beef, seasoned with salt and grilled over the fire on a skewer.

Ranks of gleaming new car engines
await shipment to Italy from Fiat's
giant factory at Belo Horizonte, capital
of Minas Gerais. Fiat arrived in Brazil
in 1974, soon after General Motors,
Ford and Volkswagen, and by 1980 the
"big four" together were producing
over one million cars per year.

AN ECONOMIC ROLLER COASTER

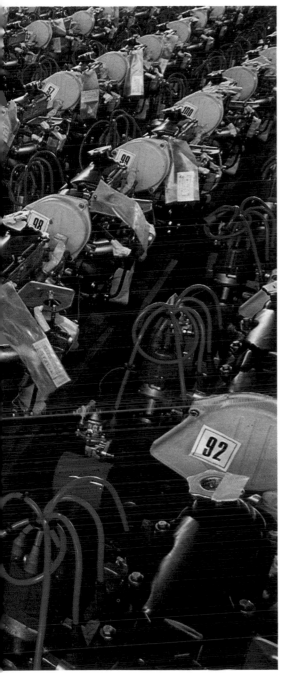

It is more than 400 years since the last foolhardy adventurers to sail up the Amazon in search of Eldorado vanished beneath the river's impassive surface. Yet the conviction that Brazil's vast hinterland offers riches beyond measure dies hard among the gamblers of the world, and in 1967 their number was swelled by Daniel K. Ludwig, an American multimillionaire and entrepreneur. Ludwig's Eldorado was made of paper, not gold: he planned to capture a large part of the world market in wood pulp. In the first phase of a grandiose $700 million scheme, he bought 1.5 million hectares of Amazon forest along the Jari river, floated a complete pulp-making factory half-way round the globe from Japan, and planted millions of saplings of what he believed to be the world's fastest-growing tree, the gmelina, which originated in the rainforests of Asia.

To cover his options and so fully exploit the resources of his Jari property, Ludwig also planned the world's largest rice paddy and the world's largest palm tree plantation. A mixed farming operation would produce crops including sugar, maize, manioc and castor oil, while 50,000 head of cattle would graze on a massive ranch. Nor did Ludwig forget the riches beneath the soil: gold, diamonds, tin and bauxite were the genies in the bottle which would finance the entire project.

By 1980 Jari had a work force of 7,000, with its own schools, hospitals, harbour and airport. But two years later, the Amazon claimed one more in a long line of victims. The cost of pulping had proved higher than anticipated; the super-tree had failed to grow fast enough, or had simply died in the dry season; and the costs of mining and farming were astronomic. With losses mounting to $75 million, Ludwig, once reported to be the world's richest man, disposed of 40 per cent of his dream to a Brazilian entrepreneur, and the remainder to a consortium of bankers, financiers and construction companies, who then proceeded to considerably scale down the project. By the mid-1980s, the Jari project was just breaking even, but nowhere near paying off its fearsome debts.

Taken in isolation, the rise and fall of Ludwig's aspirations was only one of many similar dreams of wealth that have been disappointed during the history of Brazil's development. Time and again, ignoring basic development, the nation has pinned all its economic hopes on one single export commodity, only to see the market collapse, leaving it to search desperately for an alternative. For 400 years, this narrow ambition has taken the entire country—leaders, speculators, citizens and slaves—on a desperate, unending roller-coaster ride of boom and bust. In the 1970s, Brazil reached the very brink of glory when, after 20 years of astonishing growth, the nation appeared to be slipping through the eye of the economic needle to take its place among the major powers.

Brazil achieved its industrial transformation in a very short time. From the modest industrial base established by President Getúlio Vargas in the 1930s, it made two huge strides into industrialization: the first between 1947 and 1961, under democratic government, the second between 1968 and 1974, under military government. In that last period alone the economy grew by 50 per cent, and reached a staggering 14 per cent growth rate in 1973, the peak year. Growth continued more steadily after that right up to the end of the decade, when Brazil was able to claim that it had more than quadrupled its economy in size from $45 billion to $205 billion. It was now the eighth largest economy in the Western world and was in the top 10 for steel production, electricity generation, motor car manufacture and ore mining. It also became the world's third largest food producer, after the United States and France.

But in 1980, the boom ended with a resounding crash that left Brazil the world's greatest debtor, owing 700 overseas banks a total of $100 billion—$833 for every man, woman and child in the country. In all but proportion, this spectacular collapse, which would have threatened the economy of the entire Western world had Brazil reneged on its debts, was no more than another familiar instance of economic failure in a whole series that have recurred throughout Brazil's history. In Brazil, it seems, the alternative to full-scale success is utter ruin.

Ever since the Portuguese colonized this vast territory in the 16th century, Brazil has exploited its resources one by one, going from monoculture to monoculture. Whatever crop was likely to fetch a high price on the world's markets was planted on a huge scale: alternative crops were ignored, and the development of a solid base of mixed farming was neglected because it did not yield the high profits expected by Brazil's plantation owners. But the price of their short-sighted opportunism was a profound vulnerability to sudden shifts in international demand.

The first boom, built on sugar cane planted, reaped and milled by thousands of African slaves, started in the 17th century and went bust in the 18th century when slaves on Caribbean and North American plantations began to produce the crop more cheaply. The second, the gold rush in the state of Minas Gerais at the end of the 17th century, brought a shift in population from the north to the south of the country, but foundered a century later when the gold seams were exhausted. However, the profits from mining financed the third and longest-lasting boom: coffee. The beans were first planted in the 1790s in the state of Rio de Janeiro, and later round the worked-out goldfields of Minas Gerais. By 1845, almost half the nation's export earnings came from coffee, the continued growth of which stimulated a further bout of immigration— 800,000 new settlers arrived between 1870 and 1900, three quarters of them from Italy, the rest from Portugal, Germany and central Europe.

The age of coffee was punctuated briefly by a world demand for the natural rubber of Amazonia, at that time the only known source. The rubber boom began in the last quarter of the 19th century, after the pneumatic tyre was invented, but collapsed in 1913, undermined by Britain's Malayan plantations, themselves grown from rubber seeds smuggled out of Brazil. The speculators who had swarmed up the river in the 1880s departed within three decades.

Luckily for the Brazilian economy, there was a growing demand for coffee, and production rose steadily to a peak of 28.5 million sacks in 1930—about the level it remains today. At the same time, Brazil's coffee barons and investors from Britain and the United States were taking the first tentative steps towards building an elementary industrial infrastructure. The Brazilian government borrowed huge sums to build railways and ports; gas and electricity were installed in some of the larger cities. So, when the world recession in 1929 triggered a collapse in the price of coffee, the familiar elements of a Brazilian economic crisis were all neatly in place: a large foreign debt and total dependence on a single crop.

Now, at last, the solution to the country's recurring economic problems began to dawn on the government and Brazil's financial élite: the hair-raising cycle of boom and bust would never be broken until Brazil could diversify her agricultural production and build up a manufacturing industry strong enough to ride out setbacks in any one sector of the economy. Moreover, Brazil also had to create a domestic market large enough to maintain a minimum demand for its goods during periods of recession. To create a sound industrial base, the country would need further investment, funded by still more borrowing from abroad; to develop a market, Brazil would need a well-paid work force with cash to spend. The trouble was that 90 per cent of Brazil's population, 42 million people at the start of World War II, were unpaid peons working on plantations in conditions little better than slavery, or were peasants scratching a subsistence living from the country's least productive land.

The rush for industrial growth began in earnest under Getúlio Vargas, who seized power in October 1930 and ruled Brazil almost continuously until 1954. Modelling himself to some extent on Italy's Benito Mussolini, and ruling by decree, Vargas established state-controlled, and therefore pliable, trade unions, and ploughed state capital into cornerstone enterprises such as the country's first steel mill, which opened at Volta Redonda in 1946, a National Development Bank and the

oil-refining monopoly Petrobras, both inaugurated in the early 1950s.

Vargas' contribution to Brazil's development as an industrial nation was considerable, but he was building on a very low base, and when he left office in 1954 much remained to be done to unlock the massive resources of the country's hinterland. One of the main weaknesses was communications: the railways could hardly be described as a system, still less a network, connecting, as they did, only a few scattered areas inland from the main ports. Roads were rudimentary, usually little more than unpaved tracks vulnerable to the weather. Inland journeys could take on epic proportions during the

rainy season, when fords became impassible and flimsy bridges made from tree trunks were swept away. Passengers on buses would prepare themselves with food and clothing for journeys which could take weeks, during which they often had to dismount and help dig out a vehicle buried in mud. It was not uncommon for truck drivers to carry guns so that, if they were stranded on the road, they could go hunting for wild game to eke out their provisions. It was much easier to travel by ship than by road from Belém or Recife, in the north-east, to Rio or São Paulo, in the central-south.

When Vargas' successor as president, Juscelino Kubitschek, came to

4

power in 1956, he immediately turned his attention to Brazil's communications problems. As Governor of the state of Minas Gerais during the Vargas years, he had given priority to hydroelectric power and road building, and, as national leader, he extended that priority right across the country. The keystone of his plan was to move the capital from Rio de Janeiro, on the coast, to a place closer to the centre of the country—a bare tract of scrubland in the state of Goiás. It was to be the focal point of a huge network of roads that would unite Brazil's distant frontiers and integrate its development as an industrial nation.

Kubitschek also commissioned the 1,700-kilometre-long Belém-Brasília Highway, much of it hacked clear across the Amazon forest to provide the country's first all-year route to the north. In addition, he took the first steps towards establishing a mass consumer industry. With new roads, there was new demand for vehicles: Vargas encouraged a local motor industry to expand production, and soon Ford, General Motors, Volkswagen and Fiat were among the biggest employers. The populations of the cities swelled enormously as peasants from the north-east left the land in droves, heading south to find jobs in construction or in the new industries that were springing up in the "ABCD" suburbs of São Paulo—Santo André, São Bernardo, São Caetano and Diadema.

The price of Kubitschek's achievement, however, was a massive increase in borrowing from abroad and rampant inflation: problems that were inherited by the Presidents of the two short-lived governments that followed. Both Presidents found themselves caught between the conflicting wishes of Brazil's international creditors, who wanted to see a more realistic approach to the management of the Brazilian economy, and the growing class of industrial workers, who objected increasingly vociferously to the implied squeeze on wages and living standards.

The first of Kubitschek's successors, Jânio Quadros, tried to please the bankers and the International Monetary Fund, and his government fell after less than a year in office. The second, João Goulart, a left-wing populist, tried to appease the trade unions, and inflation soared. In 1964, trade unions, middle-class radicals in the cities and left-wing peasant leagues were becoming vociferous in their demands for political and agrarian reform. There were demonstrations and mutinies in the armed forces, and the economy showed signs of faltering. On April 1, 1964, a group of army generals, convinced that the country had become ungovernable and that the leftward swing of politics had gone far enough, took control of Brazil.

The austerity of the first period of military government soon gave way to repression as strikes were all but outlawed and union leaders were thrown into prison. There was no more collective bargaining: the state, not the bosses and the unions, decided what pay rises would be given. Increases were announced just once a year: an austerity measure in itself when inflation was running at 80 per cent. At the same time, credit was severely controlled, which resulted in a decrease in domestic demand; tax collection was tightened up; and indexation was introduced—a mechanism that linked all prices and costs to the rate of inflation. As the inflation rate fell from 80 to 25 per cent in just two years, so wage rises, rents, public service charges and transport costs all fell in turn.

Yet the military had no intention of abandoning growth as a goal. If anything, their vision of Brazil's future was the most grandiose ever: to make Brazil a front-rank world power by the year 2000, negotiating on equal terms with the United States, Western Europe and Japan. They appointed Antônio Delfim Netto, a technocrat who had made a brilliant reputation as Professor of Economics at the University of São Paulo, to usher in "the decade of the miracle". A born optimist and *bon vivant*, Delfim had a personality to match his substantial girth and brought his exuberance into national affairs. A group of economists, known as "Delfim's boys", soon took up key positions in the power network.

The dynamic Delfim was quick to realize that conditions were extremely favourable to tempt foreign capital into Brazil. Throughout the industrial world, corporations were beset by the soaring costs of labour, energy and materials. Brazil could offer them all three commodities at very competitive rates, as well as a domestic market that was estimated to reach 30 million wage earners by the year 1985. All that the country needed was capital; and this the foreign companies could bring themselves, or local firms could borrow from abroad.

The economy boomed, giving plenty of scope for Brazilians to profit. For the rich, there were constant opportunities for investment and reinvestment in industry, and the profits were handsome—because capital gains were (and still are) untaxed. As the cities expanded, everyone who was anyone bought a second or third weekend home on the coast or in the mountains near the cities; fortunes were made from buying and selling land and property development. Cement production, spurred on by the construction bonanza, grew between 1970 and 1980 from 9 million tonnes to 27 million. Industry increased its output by 233 per cent between 1970 and 1979, commerce by 211 per cent and transport by 215 per cent. The motor industry alone more than trebled production from 416,000 vehicles in 1970 to 1.6 million in 1980, while the output of trucks shot from fewer than a million a year in 1970 to almost three million in 1980. At the same time a spectacular road-building programme went ahead, drawing the farthest corners of the country together, including the 4,300-kilometre Trans-Amazonian Highway, which was carved through virgin forest clear across Brazil from east to west. The only laggard was agriculture, which registered a relatively modest 156 per cent increase during the decade.

On that kind of economic growth, Brazil became the world bankers' favourite investment prospect. Loan money poured into the country from abroad despite several cautionary signals which the lenders somehow failed to heed. The first was the world oil crisis of 1973, when the price of crude sprang from $2 a barrel to more than $12, pushing up the price of goods in the industrialized nations and doubling Brazil's import bill. At the same time commodity prices plunged, which brought down the value of Brazil's exports. But, by that time there was a glut of money entering the world's banking system from the Middle Eastern countries, now fabulously rich from their oil sales. The money had to be put to use somewhere, and with Europe and the United States deep in

Shielded from the scorching sunlight by a blue plastic canopy, thousands of tender coffee seedlings flourish in the red soil of Paraná. One tenth of all Brazilians earn their living from coffee and the nation is by far the world's largest producer, growing more than 30 per cent of the total harvest.

At the Areia Branca salt pans in Rio Grande do Norte, sea water is channelled into shallow ponds and left to evaporate in the sun. When the surface turns a pale reddish colour, the remaining water is drained off, exposing a crust of salt crystals which are raked into heaps to dry at the edge.

recession, Brazil was one of the best investment prospects in the world.

In 1974, General Ernesto Geisel, an austere and authoritarian soldier, became President. But the blueprint for development scarcely changed: the national plan announced that year gave a further boost to steel, non-ferrous metal and chemical production, as well as new investment in railways to carry increased tonnages of ores and processed metals. A contract was signed with West Germany for eight nuclear power stations, complete with fuel processing plants. The estimated cost of the project, the biggest export order Germany had ever had, was $18 billion, but, with interest payments on borrowing from international banks to pay for the project, the final figure Brazil would have to pay was estimated at closer to $30 billion.

A few sceptical voices from the political left, the universities and independent research centres warned that the economy had become dangerously overheated, but they were shrugged off by the military leadership. Then, as international interest rates began to climb, new borrowing was required just to keep pace with debt-servicing commitments, and, in 1975, the government was forced to put the first cautious controls on foreign loans. Aimed mainly at dampening the foreign borrowing of importers, these measures mainly affected the private sector: the state monopolies in energy production, minerals and transport, which all had a large number of uncompleted development projects, continued to borrow unhindered. In 1972, two thirds of foreign loans had been made to private industry; only seven years later, however, two thirds of all new borrowing was done by the state.

The crunch came in 1979 when, as a result of the second world oil crisis, Brazil's import bill was pushed up once again, this time by $4 billion, creating a trading deficit of $3 billion, and an overall deficit, including loans, of $15 billion. When Brazil requested more cash to service the debt, overseas bankers discovered in the small print of their house rules such restrictions as "country limits"—the maximum proportion of their total lending that could be made to any one country. The bankers refused all further credit and Brazil found itself teetering on the verge of bankruptcy.

The crash hit the pockets and the jobs of ordinary Brazilians with bewildering speed, and the political consequences were quick to follow. But the greatest blow was to Brazilian pride. Everything had seemed to be going so well: the country was trading with an ever-widening number of nations, and its international political clout was growing. In a decade of growth, the paid work force had doubled to 14.3 million people, incomes for nearly everyone in employment had risen, and the "trickle down" effect of spreading wealth was just beginning to improve the conditions of the masses of Brazilians living in poverty. Now Brazil was forced to go, cap in hand, to the International Monetary Fund, ad-

mit that it had failed to run its own economy properly, and ask for help.

The IMF's conditions were tough and followed the classic formula for restoring economies to health: cut imports, increase exports and slash domestic consumption. Many Brazilians were outraged. Such a solution, they argued, might be suitable to a developed nation, but for a country like theirs, poised on the threshold of the First World, it was ruinous; what was needed was further growth to expand the domestic market and bring more people into the economy. In addition, with Brazil's ever-increasing population, 1.5 million jobs had to be created each year just to stay level on the unemployment percentages. In high circles there was talk of Brazil declaring a unilateral moratorium on its debts, cocking a snook at the international bankers, and working out its own economic salvation in isolation.

In the event, more sober counsel prevailed, and Brazil accepted the IMF's conditions. The *cruzeiro* was devalued by almost a third, wages were squeezed and the prices of essentials such as fuel oil, electricity, gas, transport and postal services were all raised. Food subsidies, earlier introduced to help the poor with mounting inflation, were phased out. As the chill wind of parsimony blew into every corner of the Brazilian economy, industry and commerce had to endure considerable belt-tightening.

In 1981, and again in 1983, the economy actually shrank, with industrial production declining by at least a fifth, and unemployment and underemployment standing at over 30 per cent of the work force. In São Paulo, "the locomotive that pulls the rest of Brazil", the Federation of Industries

stated in 1983 that its member industries had reduced their manpower by 40 per cent in the last couple of years, and that there were now only as many industrial workers in the state as there had been a decade previously. The civil construction industry, one of the most important employment ladders for migrants to the cities, employed only half as many workers in 1983 as it had done a decade before. And for those who were out of work, there was no unemployment benefit to tide them through the difficult times.

By 1984, wages had fallen to the level of seven years earlier and matters were made even worse by inflation, which, during the first half of the 1980s, usually exceeded 100 per cent and often peaked at more than 200 per cent. During this period, the numbers of people living in *favelas* doubled in places like São Paulo as new immigrants to the cities failed to find work and industrial workers lost their jobs. The middle classes, too, were by no means exempt from hardship, and their living standards tumbled.

Cracks in the fabric of urban society began to appear in 1983 when crime increased sharply. That year the 2,840 murders reported in São Paulo alone made it one of the world's most violent cities. Burglary also reached epidemic proportions, but the most alarming development came in April 1983 when hundreds of supermarkets in cities all over Brazil were sacked and looted by rampaging mobs, whose main motive was simple hunger.

This was the first clear warning to the military government that time was running out. The patience of the masses could no longer be taken for granted. For nearly two decades the Brazilian working class had been

4

remarkable for its political passivity: indeed, this had been one of the aspects of the Brazilian economy that had attracted foreign investors. Much of this apparent stoicism about poor wages and working conditions owed itself to the optimism of the miracle decade when industrial workers felt that, if they kept on trying and working hard at their jobs, they would progress up the ladder. Now the miracle was over, the hope was gone and the sacrifices they were being asked to make seemed much less reasonable.

Popular pressure for the economic cake to be shared out more fairly mounted as the cake itself shrank. At the end of 1984, a flurry of industrial protest led by the embryo left-wing PT, the Workers' Party, signalled the end of the era of docile trade unions inaugurated by Vargas in the 1930s. A new breed of leaders had emerged, encouraged by the example of the charismatic Luiz Inácio da Silva— better known as Lula.

One of the hundreds of thousands of peasants who had made the trek down from the north-east on the back of an open truck, Lula was a fiery and accomplished public speaker who seemed instinctively to express the fears and aspirations of his fellow workers. Described by one of his opponents as "a force of nature", he had first made his mark as president of the São Bernardo Metalworkers' Union, whose 42-day strike in 1980, for a 15 per cent wage increase, had taken the employers and the government utterly by surprise. Troops were sent in, Lula and 16 other leaders were arrested, and Lula was subsequently sacked from the union leadership. Although charges of inciting an illegal strike hung over him for several years, Lula still succeeded in

MANAUS' MAGNIFICENT FOLLY

Sixteen hundred kilometres up the Amazon, in a town surrounded by rainforest, stands one of the world's grandest opera houses—a fantastic relic of the rubber boom which shook this sleepy river port into vigorous life between 1880 and 1913. The huge profits made from Brazilian latex produced an instant plutocracy of rubber barons, who demanded all the trappings of European luxury.

Manaus soon boasted public gardens, billiard rooms, a race course and a bullring, but the town's crowning civic extravagance was its opera house, the Teatro Amazonas. The finest artists and craftsmen of Europe supplied its elegant fittings: paintings from Rome, chandeliers from Venice, roof tiles from Alsace, wrought iron from Glasgow, were all shipped up the Amazon to Manaus.

On opening night in 1896, some 1,600 patrons took their seats beneath the pink cherubs cavorting on the theatre ceiling. The gentlemen wore evening suits cleaned and pressed in Lisbon; the ladies sparkled with diamonds, for during the boom years more gems were sold in Manaus than anywhere else in the world.

Yet no full-length opera was ever staged at the Teatro Amazonas. Although some theatrical stars of international calibre were lured there by huge fees, the management persuaded few performers to risk the perilous journey through the fever-ridden rainforest.

In 1913, when plantations in South-East Asia began producing latex, Manaus' boom collapsed. The rubber barons were ruined and the opera house was closed. Since 1967, however, when the port was declared a duty-free zone, commerce has revived, bringing renewed hopes that the building will at last be put to its intended use.

Art nouveau chandeliers light the foyer of the theatre, which was fully renovated in 1974.

Lovingly restored but rarely used, the imposing Manaus Opera House overlooks the Praça São Sebastião, paved in a traditional mosaic. A 19th-century monument commemorates the opening of Manaus to foreign shipping in 1868, when the Amazon port was little more than a village.

An allegorical painting of river gods decorates the drop curtain used between acts.

4

forming the PT, a radical political grouping, which, by 1984, had spread all over the country, and was attracting support not only from industrial workers, but also from peasants and middle-class radicals.

The military government was now convinced that its economic strategy was failing and that the attempt to meet the terms laid down by the IMF was impossible to sustain. For 21 years it had governed in relative peace on the promise of achieving economic progress, but now there was real danger of a complete breakdown in law and order, if not of revolution; and the military no longer had the will to crush dissent, or even to rule. In the spring of 1985, a civilian administration prepared to take over, with Táncredo Neves, the President-elect, promising growth, prosperity and an end to the slump. It was a promise which clearly contained a veiled threat of rescheduling Brazil's massive international debt, or even of declaring a moratorium on repayments. "Brazil's debt cannot be paid with people's hunger," declared the ailing Neves, who died before taking office. And his successor, President José Sarney, echoed the same defiant message.

The restoration of democracy in March 1985 was greeted by a wave of popular enthusiasm and relief throughout Brazil. "Democracy" was the theme of Carnival in several cities, and even the untimely death of Tancredo Neves, upon whom most Brazilians had pinned their hopes, could not dampen the revived spirit of national optimism which had swept the country. As far as the new government was concerned, this new mood at least removed the pressing problem of

rumbling revolt and social breakdown which had brought down its predecessors. A further breathing space came from the IMF, who gave the government time to take stock and come up with a new solution to the problem of Brazil's international indebtedness.

In fact, the military government's balance sheet of economic achievement was by no means all bad, nor had the progress of the "miracle decade" been wasted. It had been the generals who, soon after assuming power in 1964, had taken the first steps towards integrating the external and internal sectors of the economy with the creation of official agencies to stimulate the development of the more backward regions. SUDECO and SUDESUL were set up to concentrate on the centre-west and the south, SUDENE and SUDAM had the more difficult task of the north-east and the Amazon. Success, however, had been patchy. In the backward north-east, where a quarter of Brazil's population live, SUDENE had created little new employment, and in 1985 almost half the population there still earned less than $100 a month: a negligible amount when required for the support of an average family of six children. In Amazonia, SUDAM was heavily criticized for its support of large ranching operations and settlement programmes that had subsequently failed, but it did earn some applause for backing large-scale new mineral projects.

In the main, however, the development boards were prime examples of a massive state bureaucracy that grew up under the generals—a bureaucracy whose corruption, incompetence and ostentation became a national byword. Despite the appointment of a Minister of Debureaucratization, the state sec-

tor had become so bloated by the mid-1980s that it was running no fewer than 500-odd state enterprises, that together made up over half the country's economy.

The continuing emphasis upon the public sector—curious, to say the least, under a regime committed to free-enterprise capitalism—was very palpable. Unlike the United States or Europe, where the headquarters of major private companies are invariably vast, luxuriously appointed and far more prominent than those of public bodies, the prime sites in Brazil's cities were occupied by the headquarters of dozens of state corporations, which had their buildings designed by the country's best architects, had the largest and most conspicuous offices, and the brightest, prettiest and best-dressed secretaries.

In Rio de Janeiro, a trio of three massive office blocks—the offices of the National Development Bank, the National Housing Bank, and Petrobras, the state-owned oil company—stood grouped together in splendid isolation on a prime central site. In the capital, Brasília, the most lavish building of all was the Central Bank, a soaring, elegant tower of tinted glass, its sheer heights broken by hanging gardens. Ministers and top officials lived like tycoons, occupying palatial residences along the lakeside, and vying with each other for the largest number of staff and the biggest swimming pools. The highest in the pecking order had their own jets, or called on the Air Force to whisk them from one end of the country to the other.

Inevitably, bureaucratic disregard for the finer points of commercial viability, combined with the generals' grandiose vision of Brazil's future,

In a campaign to cut oil imports, a poster urges Brazilians to fuel their cars with alcohol distilled from sugar cane. The sign carries two warnings: do not mix with petrol, and do not use in unconverted engines. Nearly half of all Brazilian cars use the new fuel.

had resulted in expensive "white elephants". The nuclear programme, which had cost $2.5 billion by 1985, had ground to a halt, with only two of the contracted eight power stations likely to be completed. A "Steel Line" railway, planned to link the iron ore mines of Minas Gerais with the steel mills of São Paulo, Rio de Janeiro and the ports, had been abandoned after $2 billion had been spent on preparing the bed of the railway and cutting through the mountains. After the unfinished line had been allowed to fall into disrepair, it was found that existing lines could cope quite easily with the volume of traffic. Many people also doubted that the $131 million spent on the Trans-Amazonian Highway could ever be justified: not only were sections of it continually being washed away in tropical rainstorms, but it also ran parallel to the Amazon river, a natural transport artery.

One of the military government's greatest mistakes had been in failing to develop agriculture in step with industry. During the "miracle decade" there had been a 13 per cent rise in the output of crops for export, but only a 1.7 per cent increase in domestic food production. After two decades which had seen a considerable growth of population, the amount of food, including staples such as maize, beans, rice and manioc, that was available for each Brazilian had declined by a fifth. The problem the generals had failed to address was the oldest in Brazilian economic history: an excessive emphasis on growing cash crops for export at the expense of developing a broadly based agricultural economy.

During the military rule, the new fashionable crop of Brazil's agribusinessmen was soya. In 14 years soya production increased eightfold, until it reached 16 million tonnes in 1984 and earned $3 billion in exports, mainly to the United States. But by 1985 the basic law of supply and demand sent prices tumbling, and it seemed the soya bean would be joining the long list of export crops that have gone bust

ÁLCOOL hidratado

1. Não misturar à gasolina.
2. Não utilizar em motores não adaptados.

4

in Brazil. In the meantime domestic food production languished, remaining disproportionately concentrated in the south, where a relatively small number of farmers of European stock, and with a European tradition of mixed farming, were settled.

Another major agricultural challenge that the military government had failed to confront was inequality of land distribution—a problem that owed its origins to the 17th century and the plantation families who spent much of their energies in consolidating huge land holdings. In the 1980s, half the country's best arable land was still in the hands of barely 1 per cent of the landowners, and their huge plantations, which were sometimes underused or not cultivated at all, provided the barest income for a vast army of some nine million landless agricultural labourers. The next 9 per cent of farmers had a third of the land, and the other 90 per cent, usually subsistence peasants, owned less than a fifth.

For President Sarney's democratic government, the long-term agricultural prospects looked very bleak. Turning the millions of landless labourers into skilled farmers was itself a daunting task. And when the government announced a programme of land redistribution to peasant settlers, the plantation landowners reacted in fury. Although the land reform proposal offered generous compensation for all land to be expropriated, the landowners wanted none of it, and they wielded one of Brazil's most powerful lobbies; so formidable was this lobby that even the military government, which had also recognized the urgency of land reform, had baulked at confronting it.

The most valuable legacy of 21 years of military rule was the huge improvements that had been made to the country's infrastructure. Most of this had been financed by borrowing from abroad, but at least it can be said that the country's $100 billion foreign debt has been mostly well spent. The Trans-Amazonian Highway may be a disappointment, yet elsewhere a network of roads now reaches into the remotest corners of Brazil's hinterland, and great strides have been made in harnessing the country's hydroelectric potential, calculated as the fourth largest in the world.

In 1984, the first of 18 massive turbines started to turn at the $18 billion Itaipu Dam, the world's largest, on the Paraná river which marks the border of Paraguay and Brazil. Itaipu is intended to generate enough power to satisfy the projected industrial needs of São Paulo and Rio de Janeiro until the end of the century. The Tucurui Dam in Amazonia is equally impressive, holding back the Tocantins river, a tributary of the Amazon, with one of the longest barrages ever built. Opened in 1984, the Tucurui Dam is designed to power the nearby Carajás mining complex, which boasts one of the world's largest deposits of iron ore, as well as large amounts of aluminium and other metals.

These two giant projects are a key element in opening the way to the exploitation of Brazil's massive and still largely untapped mineral wealth. For many years geologists have guessed at their existence, but Brazil still lags far behind other mineral-producing countries in accurately mapping its underground riches. This is partly because much of the land has been leached by extreme tropical weather conditions which obscure tell-tale surface traces of minerals, but also many

This dusty hillside at Carajás, in the Amazonian forest, conceals the world's largest iron mountain, discovered in 1967 when a geologist was forced to land his helicopter on the top. Carajás has reserves of over 18,000 million tonnes of iron ore, and large deposits of bauxite, manganese and copper.

of them are hidden beneath impenetrable rainforest. In addition, mining has proved uneconomic on account of the lack of infrastructure, the expense of importing skilled manpower, and the distance from the markets.

Until fairly recently, these difficulties have deterred international mining companies from exploiting Brazil's riches. However, spurred on by the discovery of Carajás' iron ore and bauxite, many companies have been quietly expanding their prospecting programmes, and it is now thought that Brazil has huge deposits of nearly all commercially mined minerals—the exceptions appear to be metals in the platinum group, cobalt and vanadium.

The availability of cheap electricity, which is crucial to the smelting process, has given additional impetus to mineral extraction, and in 1984 Brazil surpassed Australia as the world's largest iron ore exporter. Exploitation of the country's huge bauxite resources is also now going rapidly ahead: a Brazilian-Japanese consortium and an Anglo-American company have started separate smelting plants in Amazonia, which are expected to be producing between them a total of one million tonnes of aluminium annually before the end of the 1980s. In addition, Brazil is also looking for ways of profiting by its proven reserves of 300,000 tonnes of uranium—one of the largest known deposits in the world—which were mainly discovered after the initiation of Brazil's ill-fated nuclear power programme.

Not all of Brazil's minerals are being extracted and processed by big companies. In Amazonia, where gold is usually found in small, isolated alluvial deposits, and where the difficulties of the terrain often make large-scale mining impossible, an army of half a million independent diggers are searching for gold through the mud and sand of hundreds of hillsides and rivers. Many die from tropical diseases, in accidents, or in fights with rivals or Indians who object to the prospectors' encroachment on their territories. But, as a result of their efforts, Brazil's output of gold rose dramatically from about five tonnes a year in 1979 to over 50 tonnes in 1985. If the world gold price stays high enough to make it sufficiently worthwhile for the prospectors, the country's gold output could reach between 70 and 100 tonnes annually, which would rank Brazil as the world's second largest gold producer, behind South Africa.

Brazil's most outstanding achievement has been to go most of the way towards solving its oil problems. It was the 1979 world oil price rise that had caused the country's financial crisis by pushing its import bill beyond an acceptable point; in 1981, the country was still spending a huge $10.5 billion on importing oil, a sum which nearly wiped out its export earnings, but the search had already started for alternative sources of fuel, and for oil itself.

At first, oil exploration, spread out along Brazil's Atlantic seaboard, yielded significant but not spectacular amounts. In 1982, however, a field called the Campos Basin, situated between 80 and 120 kilometres offshore from Rio de Janeiro, began delivering oil and gas; by 1985, production topped 600,000 barrels a day, lifting Brazil to number three among the Latin American oil producers, after Mexico and Venezuela. At the same time, an even richer field was located in the Campos Basin, and although it was 800 metres under the sea—a depth never tackled before—Petrobras sank a well into it. Brazilians were confidently predicting that oil supplies, together with other existing fuel sources, would be sufficient to meet the country's requirements by 1990.

But even the oil discoveries would not have given Brazil this promise without the contribution of a remarkable effort by the government to reduce the country's dependence on mineral fuel and find alternative sources of energy. Prodded by officials, many companies switched from oil to electricity, and even to organic fuels such as wood charcoal and sugar cane waste. But the unexpected star of the energy-substitution scheme was found above the ground in the form of alcohol distilled from humble cane sugar.

In 1984 more than nine billion litres of alcohol were produced from sugar cane, supplying 4 per cent of the country's total energy needs, and almost 90 per cent of all new cars sold in Brazil are now fitted with engines which run on the fuel. The sugar plantation owners, with the help of large government subsidies, have tripled the amount of land devoted to the crop in a decade, and now the alcohol programme replaces 120,000 barrels of oil a day and slices more than $1 billion off the annual import bill.

Despite such victories on the import side, Brazil must achieve equal success in building up its exports if it is to meet the conditions laid down by the IMF. Since 1982, the country has managed a healthy and increasing surplus of exports over imports. The export drive has been spearheaded in many cases by immigrants who moved to Brazil after the war. Industries lacking detailed knowledge of a particular part of the world find a pool of energetic sales-

In the duty-free port of Manaus, youngsters tempt tourists with trays of cheap goods, varying from socks and belts to Christmas decorations. Millions of poor Brazilian families depend on the meagre profits their children make from such petty trading.

100

men with international contacts, ready and willing to search for orders anywhere and everywhere.

One typical example is Nunzio Qaratem. Back in the early 1970s, when Brazil had a large chicken-breeding industry for home consumption but no export market, he toured his native Middle East looking for customers. At first he got nowhere: the dealers had never heard of Brazilian chicken and were reluctant to take risks. In desperation, Qaratem stretched the truth and told dealers in Abu Dhabi that he had a very good order from Iraq, which would enable him to offer them a special low rate, and so wheedled from them a trial order for 200 tonnes.

To get the chickens to his customers, Qaratem had to persuade the state shipping company, Lloyd Brasileiro, to reroute a ship specially to Abu Dhabi at great expense. But the effort paid off: Brazil exported 250,000 tonnes of frozen chicken in 1984, 90 per cent of it to the Middle East, and earned $300 million. Senhor Qaratem is now a rich man, and president of the Brazilian Association of Chicken Exporters.

Brazil's drive to export has benefited from the policy started during the military rule of shifting the country's production away from basic commodities—coffee, sugar, cocoa, cotton, iron ore and tobacco—towards manufactured and processed goods. By 1981,

manufactured goods represented 62 per cent of Brazil's total exports. Today, the major share comprises factory-made goods such as textiles, paper, vehicles, steel, shoes and a wide range of consumer goods, as well as sophisticated manufactures such as aircraft, armaments and computers.

It is on the development of an advanced technological base that Brazil has pinned its hopes for the future, and its aviation and armaments industries, built up at immense initial cost, are now mounting a challenge to advanced industrial nations. The Embraer aircraft company was set up in 1970, when the government decided it could no longer afford to import the huge

4

numbers of light planes demanded by its farmers and businessmen. Financed jointly by the government and private investors, it first concentrated on building light aircraft such as the Ipanema, which was designed for agricultural use. Embraer's first export success was the 18 to 20-seater Bandeirante passenger plane, which came on to the market in 1971. More than 400 Bandeirantes have now been sold, with the United States an important export market once the plane had won its struggle for a certificate of airworthiness, granted against fierce opposition from the U.S. manufacturers. Embraer then developed the two-seater Tucano trainer plane, named after the colourful Amazonian bird, which won a great marketing breakthrough when Britain's Royal Air Force ordered more than 130 in 1985. With a range of 12 aircraft, Embraer is now the sixth largest aircraft manufacturer in the world.

Although Brazil has had a relatively low military expenditure for years because it has avoided an arms race with its neighbours, the military government started to develop armoured cars about 15 years ago. Two versions of these, the Urutu and the Cascavel, named after poisonous snakes, are now used by the Brazilian armed forces and have also been sold to several Arab nations, who find them rugged, simple in design and easy to maintain. Brazil's fearsome Astro rocket launcher, capable of raining tonnes of Brazilian-made rockets on to a small target several kilometres away, have also been supplied to the Iraqi army. The arms industry now earns an estimated $3 billion in export sales each year.

The motor manufacturing industry has also expanded since the 1980 financial crisis. Attracted to Brazil by the cheapness of labour, the "big four" multinational car manufacturers have invested $500 million equipping factories to make the latest model world cars for sale around the globe: Brazilian-made Ford Escorts are today selling in Scandinavia cheaper than those made in Spain or Britain; General Motors ships hundreds of thousands of engines to its plants around the world; Volkswagen is planning to sell in the United States; and Fiat is exporting cars to Italy.

By 1984, the sacrifices of Brazil's wage earners and the efforts of its manufacturing and mining industries were beginning to pay off. The import bill had been cut by 15 per cent in 1981, 12 per cent in 1982, and a huge 23 per cent in 1983. In 1984 exports increased by 23 per cent, creating a record trade surplus of $12 billion—and a surge of optimism about the future. Observers predict that, with the heavy industrial base completed, scarcely any new borrowing will be needed for at least a decade, and much of what was owed abroad can be repaid.

The steel industry, for example, has more than doubled its output from 8.4 million tonnes in 1975 to 18.7 million tonnes in 1984, becoming the world's eighth largest and one of the most modern. It is now saving Brazil a fortune every year, because the cost of importing steel has shrunk from $1 billion to only $138 million in 1984. In the same time, steel exports have earned almost $9 billion, getting on for half the original $20 billion investment. The same argument is used for aluminium, tin, pulp and paper, shipbuilding and many other industries.

But there are pessimists who find equal cause for gloom. The record exports of 1984 will not be repeated, they claim, because barriers against Brazilian imports are now being raised in the United States, formerly the country's largest market. Competitors there, as in Western Europe, see Brazil as an enemy, threatening their own overseas markets and domestic industries. Although the Western nations are anxious for Brazil to pay its debts, they also fear the emergence of another Japan, which would rock the economic boat and cause them more unemployment and social problems. The pessimists predict that, until the end of the century, the country will be stuck fast on a treadmill, struggling to pay off its creditors and making no progress at all—indeed, sliding inexorably backwards—for, despite the achievement of the 1984 trade surplus, not a single cent has been knocked off Brazil's massive $100 billion international debt in five years.

It is a long time since anyone expected Brazil to become a world power by the year 2000, the goal of its military leaders in 1964. But, with its enormous resources and prodigious optimism, Brazil still promises enough to bring out the best in its people. However, the country's immediate future hangs on the whims of its creditors, not the efforts of its citizens, and few see how it can shift its immense mountain of debt. Further pressure from the world's bankers could release social and political forces that would severely shake the entire edifice of a society still only on the edge of maturity. Were that to happen, Brazil could yet turn its back on the world and attempt to go it alone. And if Brazil were to suspend its international debts, there is little anyone could do about it.

Beneath lofty trees spangled with
white lights, the streets of Salvador
are jammed with cars and buses, while
pleasure-seekers roam the boulevards.
Founded in 1549, the city was the
capital of Brazil until 1763, when it lost
its status to Rio de Janeiro.

BUILDING ITAIPU: A COLOSSUS AMONG DAMS

Photographs by Vautier-de-Nanxe, Paris

When the first turbines came into operation in 1984, the Itaipu Dam on the Paraná river between Brazil and Paraguay became the largest hydroelectric installation in the world. As part of a long-term plan to harness Brazil's immense water resources, the dam, which cost an estimated $18 billion, was intended to supply one fifth of all Brazil's electricity needs and thus reduce reliance on imported oil.

Everything about Itaipu is gargantuan: its potential daily generating capacity is enough to light a city the size of London. The dam's mighty walls are 165 metres thick and extend for 7.7 kilometres, and rest on a maze of concrete-filled tunnels. The 8.8 million cubic metres of concrete needed to construct the dam—sufficient, it is said, to build eight medium-sized towns—were supplied by three on-site cement plants and carried to the construction area in overhead wagons travelling on seven aerial cables stretched high above the dam. A town was built for the 37,000 construction workers and their families, comprising 500 housing units, four hospitals, schools for nearly 16,000 pupils, as well as cinemas and restaurants.

Itaipu is only one of several huge civil engineering projects undertaken in the last two decades in Brazil. Others include the Tucurui Dam in the north-east, the fourth largest in the world, and the 4,300-kilometre-long Trans-Amazonian Highway, which links Brazil's western frontier with the Atlantic seaboard.

Against a stormy sky, workers on the Itaipu Dam erect a web of steel reinforcement bars, which will be embedded in concrete. In recompense for arduous 11-hour shifts and a high risk of injury, the men earn twice what they would get on ordinary construction projects.

A forest of reinforcement bars, scaffolding, cranes and ladders stretches between the river banks during the building of Itaipu's powerhouse, contained in the dam's main wall. The structure will house the generators and 18 turbines, each with a daily 700-megawatt capacity.

A 10-tonne mobile crane, dwarfed by the unfinished concrete ramparts of Itaipu's main structure, is hoisted to a higher level. From its foundations on the Paraná river bed, the dam rises 224 metres, making it more than half as tall as New York's highest building, the World Trade Centre.

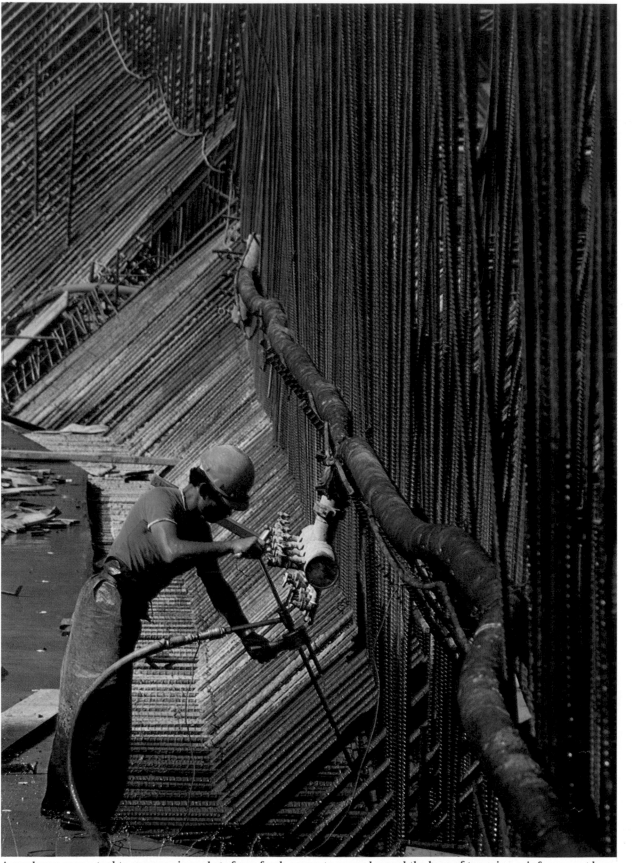

A workman uses a tool to remove air pockets from fresh concrete poured round the base of towering reinforcement bars.

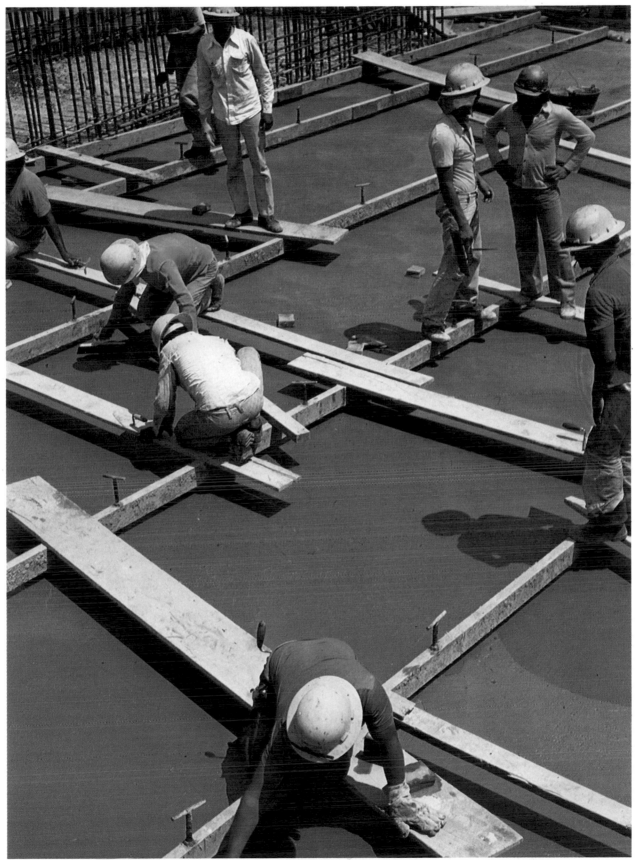

Balanced on a framework of planks, dam workers smooth down the concrete floor of the Itaipu power station.

Illuminated by the white flare of his
torch, a welder works through the
night on a massive grid of
reinforcement bars. In order to
complete the dam on schedule, work
continued right round the clock
throughout construction.

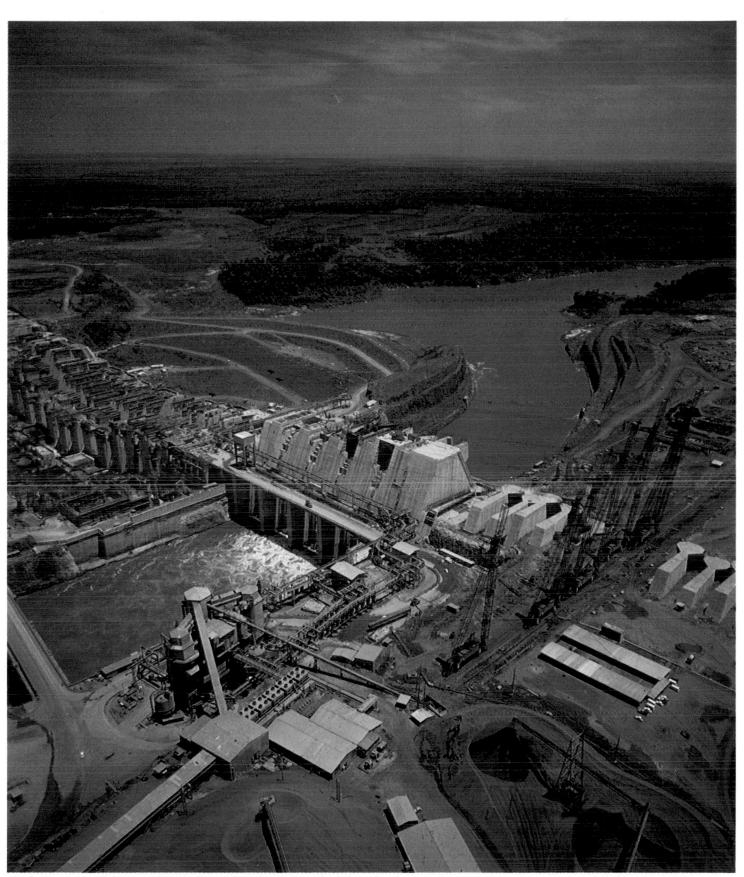

The brown water of the Paraná river, diverted during the dam building, churns through a temporary channel in the partially completed barrier.

On a patch of waste ground in Bahia, barefoot youngsters play a spirited game of football. Almost every Brazilian supports one of the country's 20,000 soccer teams, whose artistry and skill have produced many of the world's finest players and made Brazil a top footballing power.

A CULTURAL
MELTING POT

Once a year, the world is given a tantalizing glimpse of a uniquely Brazilian event, the great Dionysian revel that is Carnival in Rio de Janeiro. It has been called "the greatest show on earth", and in scale and sumptuousness it far outstrips other Christian pre-Lenten festivals such as *Fasching* in Munich, or *Mardi Gras* in New Orleans and Nice. In Rio de Janeiro, the Carnival festivities start on the Saturday before Ash Wednesday, and for the next four days and four nights the entire city abandons itself to a collective frenzy of music, dance and eroticism.

During the daytime, exotically costumed revellers parade about the streets, singing and dancing. Every evening in the theatres and night clubs, bands play Carnival music while merrymakers in fancy dress dance through the night. And on the Sunday evening there begins a gigantic parade which lasts until the afternoon of the next day. Each of the 80,000 citizens of Rio who take part belong to one of 40-odd samba schools, neighbourhood clubs which spend every weekend of the year planning and rehearsing their performance for those few hours. With big cash prizes at stake, the schools compete to create the most inspiring pageant of dancing and elaborately decorated floats.

Nowadays, Rio's Carnival is geared to the media and substantially funded by the Ministry of Tourism. The professional input in the parade's set pieces grows yearly and spontaneity correspondingly diminishes. But Brazil's other cities have their own smaller and less publicized versions of Rio's Carnival, and these are still dedicated to impromptu merrymaking. The best of the lesser carnivals are thought to be those of Salvador, Brazil's first capital, and Olinda, the colonial city adjacent to the port of Recife; there, the atmosphere is really authentic and good humour prevails.

Both Portuguese and African contributions are discernible in Carnival— but in fusing they release entirely new energies. The earliest Portuguese settlers were accustomed to letting off steam with pranks and horseplay— throwing flour or soot at their neighbours, for example—in the last few days before the onset of Lent. By the mid-19th century, however, the rough games were being replaced by religious pageants and masked balls. Meanwhile, African slaves entered into the spirit of the season, celebrating with drum music and dances—including one called the samba, which had Angolan antecedents and simulated the movements of copulation. But until well into the 20th century, this music was only one genre among many, which included guitar works and thoroughly European waltzes and polkas. Then, in 1917, a samba called *pelo telefone*—"on the telephone"—was recorded for gramophone and became an instant hit. It was the first of many

113

5

sambas to achieve renown in Brazil and beyond. Deriving from African drum rhythms and Portuguese folk songs, the syncopated music was joyful, brash and optimistic. The samba took Brazilian Carnival by storm and ever since that time has remained its most characteristic feature.

Carnival, and the samba that throbs at its heart, encapsulates Brazil's eclectic and vigorous culture. The varied heritages derived from the Brazilian population's European, African and American roots have been woven together so intricately, and transformed so radically by the shared climate, geography and social history, that something entirely new has emerged. Brazilian culture is sensuous, vital and defiantly different. Brazil's contributions to classical music, to literature and to the visual arts are by far the most significant of any South American country, and Brazilians are very well aware of the fact. But the nation's most characteristic achievements are at the popular level, the samba being the supreme example.

The confidence and great pride that Brazilians feel in their national culture is a fairly recent, 20th-century phenomenon. For most of the first four centuries after the Portuguese discovered Brazil, the inhabitants looked towards Europe for inspiration. With few exceptions, their buildings and paintings closely followed Portuguese styles, their reading matter was imported. Brazil's language was Portuguese, albeit a progressively softer and more musical version of the mother tongue, which eventually absorbed many African and Amerindian words. The Portuguese also gave Brazil its religion, and without a doubt Roman Catholi-

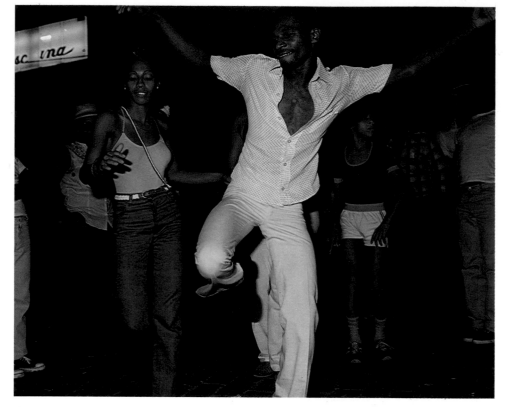

cism has been their most pervasive cultural legacy to their colony.

In the early colonial days, the Catholic Church's monopoly of ideas appeared to be virtually total. Fernando de Azevedo, in his seminal study of 1943, *Brazilian Culture*, says: "So intimate and constant are the relations between the development of religion in Brazil and that of the intellectual life in our first three centuries, that one cannot for that long period separate one from the other."

But when the first African slaves arrived in Brazil, other currents began to flow beneath the surface of society. They, too, took most powerful expression in religion. The African cults

proved as enduring as the official faith. Today, one of the most characteristic aspects of Brazilian cultural life is its blend of religions, which coexist in remarkable harmony. Brazil is the most populous Catholic country in the world, with 90 per cent of its people professing, if not actually practising, Roman Catholicism. But a growing minority, perhaps as many as 20 per cent of the population, belong to spiritist cults, and many more, while not actually belonging to a cult, participate in major spiritist festivals.

Crucially for the development of Brazil's culture, Portuguese Catholicism was never as rigid or as exigent as the Catholicism brought by the

Spanish to South America. Its lack of formality, its plasticity, left space for the absorption of other influences. This is not to say that the Church in the early days of Portuguese colonization did not attempt to impose its own cultural hegemony. Catholic missionaries, particularly the Jesuits, had indeed been ruthless about converting the Amerindians, assuming that the Indians had no art and no culture whatever, that their minds were a *tabula rasa*—a tablet scraped bare of all concepts and beliefs. The African slaves brought in to work on the sugar plantations received the same overbearing treatment. Many were baptized *en masse* by priests as they were forced on to the slave ships in African ports; in any event, they were all obliged to become Christians, and to observe Christian practices when they arrived in Brazil.

But the despised slaves brought with them their own, often sophisticated, cultures: some were adherents of old African religions with formalized rituals and pantheons. They often came from ancient polities with strong traditions of music, dance and orally transmitted poetry, where there were highly skilled sculptors who worked in wood and metal. Some of them were Muslims, and a few were more literate than their masters.

They may have crossed themselves dutifully before images of the Virgin Mary during the day, but at night they played the drums which they kept hidden in the slave quarters. In secret, they worshipped their old gods – Xangö (the god of thunder and lightning), Ogun (the god of war) and Oxössi (the god of hunters). From these practices, which were officially suppressed by the Catholic Church, was later to emerge the sorcery of Brazil's spiritist cults.

Even in Brazil's early days, Negro culture found subtle ways of infiltrating itself into the lives of Portuguese ruling classes. The black cooks who ran the kitchens of the white houses would modify traditional Portuguese and Amerindian dishes to suit

115

Cacti and scrub surround the rough home of a peasant family eking out a living in the arid interior of north-eastern Brazil. The area was the setting of Euclides da Cunha's 1902 classic of Brazilian literature, *Rebellion in the Backlands*.

their own tastes, introducing the hot peppers, okra, ginger, melon seeds and *dendé* oil of their native Africa, so creating a characteristic Brazilian cuisine. White children were reared in intimate contact with black people, who served in various domestic capacities in their houses. Black women were their wet nurses and their nannies. Black children were their childhood playmates. Black girls were their first sexual partners in boyhood, their mistresses in manhood, often their confidantes, their source of solace or special magic in time of trouble. The chief black servant of a household often gained a status not far below that of her white mistress; and the black nanny who had brought up a white child was frequently the most trusted person in that child's life for as long as she lived.

The Catholicism practised in the 17th-century sugar plantation homes was always ready to absorb these outside influences, probably not so much for liberal reasons, but more out of an amiable insouciance. The Brazilian sociologist Gilberto Freyre, in his book *The Masters and the Slaves*, describes the religion of the plantation owners as "domestic, lyric and festive Christianity, with its humanly friendly male and female saints and its Our Ladies as godmothers to the young".

It was a faith which had little interest in strict orthodoxy, but adapted itself to the daily needs and the morals of the plantation owners—and these, to say the least, were far from perfect. Padres were often the sons of plantation owners and officiated in the private chapels attached to their great houses. Very often the priests performed a valuable educational function by giving lessons to the children of the house, including the slave children;

but, like their secular peers, they quite frequently had mistresses and bastard children—and seemed unaware of any moral inconsistency.

Moral rectitude was certainly not a feature of the gold rush which followed the age of the sugar plantations, and which brought new wealth to the interior of Brazil. But one side effect of the 18th-century gold boom was a spate of magnificent church building. In the burgeoning towns of Minas Gerais, many old churches were refurbished, and many new ones were built in the baroque and rococo styles popular in Europe and particularly appropriate to the exuberant prosperity of the successful prospectors. Ringed by hills, Ouro Prêto, once known as Vila Rica, "Rich Town", and at that time capital of the region, still resembles

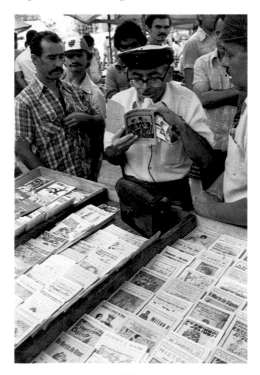

At a stall selling booklets of popular stories, a vendor entertains the crowd by giving a public reading through a microphone muffled with a handkerchief. The booklets are commonly called *cordel*, or "string", literature, from the way they used to be displayed in street markets.

Braganza or other baroque towns in northern Portugal. Its steep streets are still paved with blocks of iron slate and granite, and there are 13 splendid churches, some with interiors almost entirely covered in gold leaf.

It was in Ouro Prêto in 1738 that a genius of American colonial sculpture and architecture was born, the illegitimate child of a Portuguese carpenter and a black slave woman. His name was Antônio Francisco Lisbôa, but he is always called O Aleijadinho, "The Little Cripple", because of the progressive mutilating disease, probably leprosy, which attacked him in middle age, withered his fingers and disfigured his face.

The boy learnt his craft from his father and was soon much in demand as a sculptor of religious images and also as a church architect. As his health deteriorated he became unable to walk and his face was such a loathsome sight that he chose to work behind screens. Yet, despite his terrible afflictions, he went on working tirelessly, turning out scores of sculptures with the help of his favourite slave, Mauricio, who is said to have had to tie chisel and mallet to the stumps of O Aleijadinho's useless hands.

The results are strikingly original. Unlike other 18th-century church sculptors, O Aleijadinho did not idealize his men and women. His distorted, angular figures are reminiscent of those painted by El Greco nearly two centuries earlier. The facial features of his statues are based on those of the people—often rather frightening in their aggressiveness—who surrounded him in the harsh environment of this gold-obsessed mining town.

His masterpiece is a series of sculptures he made when he was already an old man for the Sanctuary of Bom Jesus at Congonhas do Campo, a small town near Ouro Prêto. Arrayed on the terraced forecourt of the church are 12 larger-than-life soapstone statues of the biblical prophets. And for the six chapels that line the approaches to Bom Jesus, O Aleijadinho created seven tableaux of stages in Christ's passion, all executed in life-size polychrome wood. These intense, tormented figures express the suffering in the sculptor's own life, and that of the pilgrims who, for nearly two centuries, have come to pray at the shrine.

Pilgrimage is still a powerful tradition in rural Brazil. It is an expression of the folk Catholicism of the peasants who, probably because of a perpetual shortage of priests, have retained many of the practices and superstitions of the 17th century. One famous mecca for pilgrims is the city of Bom Jesus da Lapa on the São Francisco river in Bahia: twice a year tens of thousands of people assemble here, drawn to its miracle-working image of Christ and a network of underground caverns that have been turned into shrines. Some have come on foot from as far as 800 kilometres away, to fulfil a vow or pray for divine help.

Other shrines, such as Our Lord of Bonfim in Salvador, are famous for working miracles all year round. The Bonfim has a special "museum of miracles" for votive offerings from people who have experienced faith cures. In it are wax replicas of heads, arms, legs, hearts, breasts—the parts of the body that were afflicted before a visit to the Bonfim brought about a miraculous cure. Here they also sell ribbons inscribed with the name of Our Lord of Bonfim, which are tied around the believer's left wrist. He or she can then make three wishes, which will all be granted by the time the ribbon wears away and falls off the wrist—usually a matter of three months or so—and it is a strict condition that the ribbon has to fall off of its own accord. At any given moment perhaps half the population of Salvador can be seen wearing frayed and faded ribbons. Most people maintain that their wishes have been answered, but it is important to keep them within reasonable bounds, or they may not be fulfilled after all.

Strangely, the Bonfim is also known as the church of Oxalá, the "Lord of Creation", in the pantheon of Candomblé, one of the Brazilian cults that

The foremost Brazilian composer of the 20th century, Heitor Villa-Lobos (1887–1959) works on one of his scores, cigar in mouth. A number of his world-famous compositions drew on the rhythms and melodies of Afro-Brazilian folk music and called for the use of exotic Amerindian instruments.

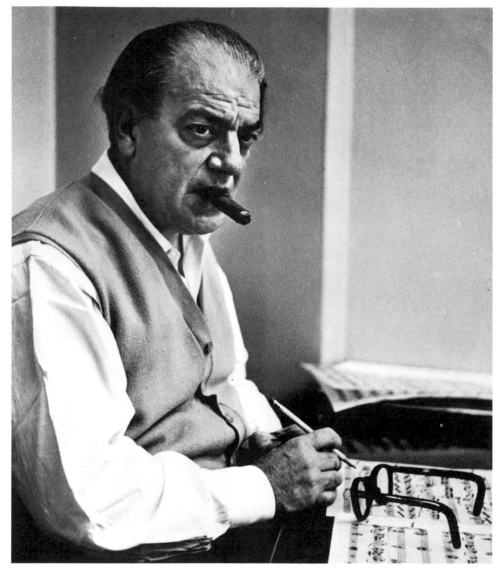

grew out of the African religions. Candomblé originated in north-eastern Brazil, among the Yoruba peoples brought from the Guinea coast of Africa; another cult, Macumba, developed in the south out of the religions of the Bantu slaves imported from Angola.

Both cults centre round media able to contact the spirit world. Practitioners may heal sickness through the aid of their familiars, or summon devils to perform black magic.

Today, Candomblé and Macumba are not confined to the descendants of African slaves or even to the poor; many highly educated, white, middle-class Brazilians slip away every month or so to attend some Afro-Brazilian magic rite. This development constitutes not so much an abandonment of Catholicism as a supplement to more orthodox religious beliefs, for many adherents of the Afro-cults remain fervent Catholics. In the Bonfim church, each January sees an important festival for members of both the Christian and Candomblé congregations, in which Catholic priests and the Candomblé spiritual leaders, who are known as "mothers-of-saintliness", walk hand in hand.

African culture, which is powerfully expressed in the religions of Brazil today, also informs some of the nation's best literature. Indeed, Brazil's first great literary figure, Antônio de Castro Alves, was himself the son of a slave. He published a volume of poems in 1870, and others appeared after his death in 1871. They expressed his anger at the hardships suffered by his people in slave ships and on the sugar plantations. He was the first really popular poet in Brazil, and his great abolitionist poem, *Voices from Africa*, is still recited in family gatherings and public meetings.

In the realm of fiction, the first important Brazilian works were written by Joaquim Maria Machado de Assis, the offspring of a black house-painter and his Portuguese wife. Machado, orphaned and epileptic, fought his way back out of the slums of Rio de Janeiro by working first as a typesetter, and then as a proofreader and journalist. As the 19th century drew to a close, he wrote a succession of novels whose sceptical and ironic tone disguised a

fine sensitivity towards the human
condition. One of the masterpieces, *The
Heritage of Quincas Borba*, tells of a man
who dissipates his fortune on a married
woman who fleeces and then deserts
him. The hero of another, *Dom Cas-
murro*, schemes for years to escape from
a seminary to unite with his childhood
sweetheart, only to endure the tortures
of an unhappy marriage.

It was left to another of the 19th-
century realists, Aluísio Azcvedo, to
produce the most powerful Brazilian
novel about the love of a black man for
a white woman, *O Mulato*. Azevedo
came from São Luís, capital of the state
of Maranhão. His account of life in São
Luís was so realistic, and was considered so scandalous at the time that he
wrote it, that he was obliged to leave
his native city and move to Rio de Janeiro. After writing two more widely
acclaimed novels he entered the diplomatic service—and never published
another book.

Castro Alves, Machado and Azevedo were figures of the Brazilian
Empire. For all their individual talent,
their work did not yet add up to a national school and the other writers
of their era tended to be strongly
Eurocentric. It was only after Brazil
became a republic in 1889 that the literary search for the country's soul began in earnest. An early pointer for the
emerging artistic nationalism was the
publication in 1902 of *Rebellion in the
Backlands* by Euclides da Cunha. His
epic account of a true event portrayed
the men who took part in it as char-
acters shaped by their labours; as pioneers in a ruthless land.

The event behind *Rebellion in the
Backlands* was an uprising in 1897 led
by the religious fanatic Antônio Maciel, known to his followers as O Conselheiro, "The Counsellor". A native
of Pernambuco, he had taken to a
nomadic, ascetic life in the backlands.
In the barren wastes 600 kilometres
from Bahia, a band of impoverished
peasants gathered round him and recognized him as their chief. They

helped him build a settlement which
was to become a Utopian community
of peace and justice. When he later
came into conflict with the Governor of
Bahia and was ordered to move, O
Conselheiro and his few thousand followers defied the authorities and

A soapstone statue of the prophet Hosea, carved by the 18th-century mulatto sculptor O Aleijadinho, "The Little Cripple", stands before a church in Congonhas do Campo. The twisted angle of the legs is believed to reflect the artist's physical deformity.

fought off the police force which had been sent to forcibly eject them.

In March 1897, some 1,500 soldiers, with four pieces of artillery, attempted to put down the rebellion, but were totally defeated. Eventually the federal government was obliged to dispatch an expeditionary force of 5,000 men to crush the rebels. Their fortress was besieged and captured in September 1897; disillusioned and despairing, O Conselheiro died shortly before the final assault.

This saga might easily have become just another footnote to Brazilian history had it not been for da Cunha, a newspaper correspondent from São Paulo who accompanied the army during the campaign. The book which he wrote about the affair has been described as the greatest of Brazilian classics and the bible of Brazilian nationality. Although the book is a work of fact, it reads like fiction. The great Viennese critic, Stefan Zweig, who spent his last years in Brazil before his death in 1942, considered that the work gave "a complete psychological picture of the Brazilian soil, the people, and the country".

Euclides da Cunha had profound sympathy and understanding for the rebellious inhabitants of the stricken north-east, who were struggling for survival in the face of a hostile environment and an uncomprehending government. He observed that these hardy frontiersmen would give every indication of overwhelming exhaustion until the very moment of having to make an effort. But: "In this weakened organism complete transformations are effected in a few seconds. All that is needed is some incident that demands the release of slumbering energies. The fellow is transfigured ... and the awkward rustic unexpectedly assumes the dominating aspect of a powerful copper-hued Titan, an amazingly different being, capable of extraordinary feats of strength and agility." Understandably, da Cunha was dismayed that such people had to die in the name of law and order, for they constituted "the very core of our nationality, the bedrock of our race."

Rebellion in the Backlands was undoubtedly a milestone, but Brazilian literature had to wait until the 1920s before it came of age. The Brazilian modernist movement arrived with a clash of cymbals in the form of manifestos and provocations such as Mário de Andrade's *Hallucinated City:* "I insult the bourgeois! O nickel-plated bourgeois, O bourgeois-bourgeois! The well-made digestion of São Paulo!" The movement culminated in a Week of Modern Art held in the city of São Paulo in 1922, to celebrate a century of Brazilian independence. Out of the many readings, exhibitions, conferences and statements of that week emerged an awareness that Brazil had something special to offer within the framework of Western culture. Writers resolved to keep up with the European avant-garde while tackling specifically Brazilian themes.

Intrigued by the primitive, as were their European and North American contemporaries, Brazilian intellectuals and literati took a sudden interest in the poorest and previously most despised of all their country's many havenots: the Indians, who lived, virtually without possessions, in the great rainforests of Brazil.

In the 19th century, a few Brazilian writers had affected a passionate interest in the Indians but it was badly informed enthusiasm: they romanticized the lifestyle of the Indians, portraying them as noble savages. Now, for the first time, Brazilians were prepared to take a realistic look at their compatriots. They recognized that the myths and music of the Indian people, their art and handicrafts, were the residual treasures of a highly complex, refined culture that had been 10,000 years in the making.

Anthropologists scoured the Indian villages, trying to record their legends and creation myths before the tale-tellers became corrupted by mass communications such as the radio. From the Tucano Indians of the north-west Amazon, for example, the anthropologists learned that: "The first men were sent to earth by the Sun Father, creator of the universe. They travelled in a great snake canoe in the form of an anaconda... These first men dispersed along the rivers and settled in the forests to people the earth."

There proved to be much to learn from these secretive peoples. Sophisticated Brazilians discovered that the Tucanos of the upper River Negro made some of the toughest, lightest and most elegant baskets in the world by skilfully plaiting together a network of jungle vines; the Kadiweu of the Paraguai river painted abstract patterns on deer hide which Picasso or Paul Klee would have admired; the Kuikuru of the Xingu river produced dance masks that might easily have been painted by Miró.

One outcome of the new respect for the Indians was the novel *Macunaíma: Hero without a Character*, by Mário de Andrade, which was published in 1928. Exploiting the racy, idiomatic language of several different regions of Brazil, it recounts the fantastic travels of its eponymous hero, a cult figure of

Indian Tupi mythology. Almost aggressively, the book asserts that Brazil has a language, a mythology and a way of life quite separate and distinct from those of Europe.

One of the most self-critical books about the Brazilian character was also written in 1928. Its author was an elderly businessman from São Paulo, Paulo Prado. His *Portrait of Brazil*, subtitled *Essay on Brazilian Melancholy*, states its thesis in a memorable opening sentence: "In a radiant land there lives a melancholy people", and develops the argument that the principal characteristics of the Brazilians are sexuality and envy. In Prado's opinion, sexual passion wore out both the Portuguese and the Indians, and from the hunger for gold there resulted the sadness of the new race, to which the African brought "his sickly collaboration as an exile and a slave".

The pessimism of Prado's book was an anomaly, and subsequent writers swung back to more joyful topics. The 1930s and 1940s saw a succession of vigorous novels and poems on Brazilian regional themes. Brazil's best known postwar novelist is Jorge Amado, whose *Gabriela, Clove and Cinnamon* celebrates the zest for life of the beautiful mulatta of the title. Every image, every personality, is drawn from Amado's birthplace—Bahia. A Communist, Amado in his earlier novels had stereotyped the virtuous and suffering peasants and the evil powermongers. But the novels of the 1950s and 1960s, such as *Gabriela, Clove and Cinnamon* and *Dona Flor and her Two Husbands*, take a more humorous view of the pretensions of the rural establishment.

Like Brazil's writers, the country's artists and musicians discovered a na-

tional identity in the 1920s. They, too, drew heavily on African traditions and self-consciously incorporated Indian motifs into their work.

It was from the Indian tribes of the Amazon and the Mato Grosso that Heitor Villa-Lobos, Brazil's foremost composer, learned the use of the exotic percussion instruments that snap, rattle and scrape in some of his instrumental compositions. In the same works, he employed African drum beats, patterns of sound which, though extraordinarily complex, never fail to set the feet moving. The alternation of African dance rhythms with the more brittle, delicate sounds of the Indian instruments is one of Villa-Lobos' characteristic hallmarks.

Although he was born in Rio de Janeiro and spent most of his life there, Villa-Lobos was drawn towards Indians and Afro-Brazilians by a musical tropism that no Brazilian composer can escape. Even when he was not employing native tambours and rattles, or trying to capture "the sounds of the jungle at night", he would base his songs and orchestral scores on the folk music he had heard in the hinterlands when he travelled through the northeast as a young man. Indeed, if any one individual can embody the *genius loci* of modern Brazil it is the prodigious Villa-Lobos; without doubt, one of the most original and versatile composers in the history of music.

By no means all of his work is dominated by percussion rhythms; much of it is subtle and elusive, such as the famous *Bachianas Brasileiras No. 5*, the fifth of his "Brazilian Tributes to the Spirit of Bach", in which a solo soprano hums a Bach-like aria to the accompaniment of eight plucked cellos, which divide up the chords between

In a canvas entitled *Café*, painted in 1934 by Cândido Portinari, a leader of Brazil's early modern art movement, workers on a coffee plantation pick, sort and carry coffee beans under the eye of a white overseer. It is a theme that expresses Portinari's lifelong concern for the poor and oppressed.

them like a giant guitar. It is a sound utterly unlike anything else to be heard in modern music. And then a contrasting *Dansa* evokes the sound of an Indian flute in the depths of the forest: "Ireré, my little nestling from the wilds of Cariri ... Sing and enchant me ... *La, lia! lia! lia! lia!*"

Villa-Lobos' career illustrates both the delights and difficulties attendant on being a composer in a land rich in musical materials but poor in financial opportunities for serious musicians. Born in 1887 of a Spanish father and a Brazilian mother, he studied cello and piano along traditional European lines before discovering the mother lode of Brazilian folk music. Soon he was writing the first experimental pieces in which Indian and Afro-Brazilian elements were joined to the Impressionist harmonies of Claude Debussy.

The trouble was that Rio had no audience for music of this sort during the early years of the 20th century. Villa-Lobos was obliged to scrape a living by playing the cello in the orchestra of a silent movie cinema. The only people who could be expected to understand his compositions were musical sophisticates from Europe who were accustomed to hearing similar experiments from composers such as Maurice Ravel and Igor Stravinsky.

One such European was the pianist Artur Rubinstein, who went to Rio on a concert tour in 1919 and happened to hear about Villa-Lobos from mutual friends. They arranged for him to be introduced to the young Brazilian composer, whom he found to be "a short man of dark complexion, clean-shaven, with dark disorderly hair and large sad eyes, but his hands were his most attractive feature with their love-ly shape, sensitive and alive". When the pianist asked whether he had writ-ten anything for the piano, Villa-Lobos said moodily: "Pianists have no use for composers. All they want is suc-cess and money."

Understandably annoyed, Rubin-stein went back to his hotel room, where, in the morning a few days later, someone knocked at his door. "I saw to my surprise 10 or 12 men carrying dif-ferent musical instruments. One of them was Villa-Lobos, who tried to convey to me in his mixed French and Portuguese that he was here to comply with my wish to hear his compositions. 'My friends are occupied during the day,' he said. 'This is the only time they are free to play.'"

It was eight o'clock in the morning, but Rubinstein agreed to listen to several of Villa-Lobos' compositions. Some were easy to understand, others difficult, but, as Rubinstein recalled, "I was convinced that I was facing a great composer."

It was the beginning of the com-poser's rise to international promin-ence, for Rubinstein also prevailed on one of Rio's wealthy art patrons to provide financial support so that Villa-Lobos could study in Paris. He went on to show the whole of Europe a new kind of dissonant, folk-based music, and after he returned to Brazil, and until his death in 1959, he was the best known and most often played South American composer.

The modernist movement of the 1920s which inspired Villa-Lobos also set off a flood of talented painters and sculptors. They kept in the vanguard of international stylistic movements but chose Brazilian themes as their subject matter. The foremost among them was Cândido Portinari. Born in 1903 in a poor Italian immigrant fam-ily, Portinari, like many Brazilian writers of the period, was fascinated by the condition of the rural poor and un-derprivileged. An immensely versatile figure, he painted most often in a sty-lized form of realism which conferred majesty even on everyday subjects. His images—coffee plantations, peasants in the north-east—were unmistakably Brazilian. From the late 1930s he was practically Brazil's official artist, being commissioned to produce many large-scale murals for the public buildings that were starting to spring up in profusion in Brazil.

Brazil's spectacular modern archi-tecture is one of the most potent ex-pressions of its 20th-century artistic confidence. In many respects, Brazil has been the architect's dream country, with ample space, relatively few building regulations and little op-position to new ideas from cautious traditionalists. A key figure in the na-tion's architectural development was Lúcio Costa, who, together with the Swiss architect Le Corbusier and other contributors, was responsible for the Ministry of Education and Culture in Rio de Janeiro. This building, com-pleted in 1942, is considered a land-mark in Brazil's architectural history.

It was Costa who, at the end of the 1950s, drew up the masterplan for Brazil's architectural showpiece, the new capital Brasília. The buildings

Near Belo Horizonte, on the rear wall of the Church of São Francisco designed by Brazil's eminent architect Oscar Niemeyer, a tiled mural portrays the life of St. Francis. Created between 1943 and 1945, by Cândido Portinari, it was at first thought as shockingly avant-garde as the church itself.

within his grand design, executed by architect Oscar Niemeyer, were acclaimed by critics and colleagues as highly original masterpieces of contemporary architecture. Excoriated by some observers as a concrete jungle lacking a human dimension, admired by others for its bold abstract forms, Niemeyer's achievement in Brasília has attracted worldwide attention.

The best Brazilian architects have refused to follow global fashions blindly. Back in the 1930s and 1940s, when the functionalist creed was being preached most insistently, a school of Brazilian architects rejected orthodoxy, espousing organic forms and attempting to integrate buildings into their natural surroundings.

Later, the native originality expressed itself in unexpected geometry. Among the most striking recent creations are Sérgio Bernades' low-slung, wheel-shaped Hotel Tambaú, which was built on the beach in João Pessoa, and Glanco Campelo's exhibition palace for the Administrative Centre of the state of Bahia—a massive concrete shape suspended in mid-air between two conical towers.

In Manaus, a brilliantly innovative architect, Severiano Mario Porto, has been building homes and offices using the native materials of the Amazon in a new and exciting way. His roofs and porches rest on rough-hewn logs from the jungle; the walls and floors are of wood or tile, resulting in a relaxed and comfortable ambience. Porto air-conditions his houses in the natural way, employing the Amazon winds for cross-ventilation, and he allows rain to fall through special openings in the roof to water his indoor gardens.

A number of other idiosyncratic Brazilian architects are providing liv-

BAHIA'S CULINARY HERITAGE

The most famous regional cuisine of Brazil is that of the north-eastern state of Bahia. Here, many distinctive dishes evolved in the kitchens of the colonial plantation owners. Because wheat flour and meat were often in short supply, their African slave cooks turned instead to the wealth of seafood caught in coastal waters and to the local produce such as manioc flour, sweet potato, coconut, pineapple and palm oil. For flavouring, they used spices from their native Africa to produce dishes such as *abará*, a mixture of prawns and black-eyed beans, and *vatapá*, a stew of fish, shrimps, ginger and coconut milk.

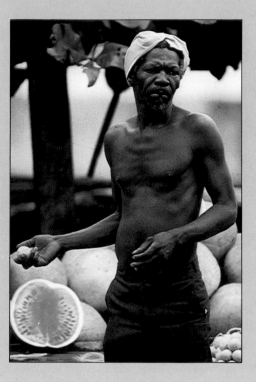

The rich variety of tropical produce is displayed on street stalls in Salvador. A man sells watermelons (*near right*); a shopper considers a purchase at a spice stall. Near the beach, tables are piled with fruits and vegetables, while two fishermen (*far right*) tempt a motorist with their lobster catch.

ing spaces as welcoming as Porto's. Zamine Cladas, for example, uses unexpected combinations of exposed concrete and local wood for his country houses, while one of the houses created by Gerson Castelo Branco, on the beach at Piauí, was inspired by the design of the region's sailing boats. Each of these architects combines thoroughly modern techniques with the priceless heritage of local materials and traditions.

Brazilian high culture is constantly drawing upon the art of the ordinary people. For, in this vast and diverse country, culture is the very stuff and substance of daily life, and by some strange law of compensation Brazil's most disadvantaged inhabitants are the possessors of some of its greatest cultural riches.

Brazil has a strong tradition of popular painting and sculpture, for example, which is barely influenced by international fashions or the burden of art-historical tradition. One of the most talented of the untutored primitives was Djanira da Mota Silva, who was a descendant of Indians and Viennese immigrants. She exhibited her work for the first time in 1942 and very quickly achieved international fame. Her strongly toned, almost two-dimensional figures and landscapes are filled with an innate lyricism. In the 1970s, another primitive artist, Iracema Arditi, drew wide acclaim for

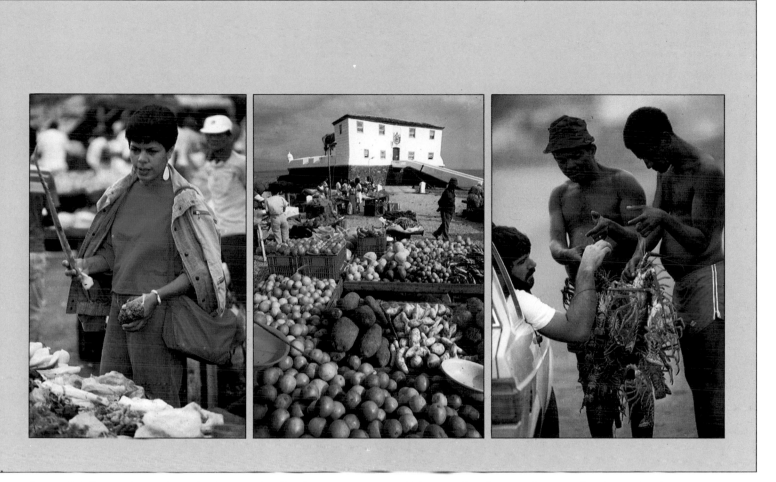

her vividly coloured paintings of flowers and tropical gardens.

But nowhere is the strength of Brazilian folk culture more obvious than in the field of popular music, which has become the country's best known art form internationally, and which draws its inspiration from a seemingly bottomless well of folk songs and dances. African influences predominate in the peculiarly Brazilian shapes and rhythms of the samba and the bossa nova, or "new skill".

The samba is simply a dance in duple time, but it is what happens to the basics that counts: the secret of its fascination lies in the syncopations, the deviations from the norm. There is a saying among Brazilian musicians:

Samba e coisa seria—"the samba is a serious matter". There are innumerable varieties of the urban as well as the rural samba—usually named for their character, instrumentation or place of origin: the *samba de viola* (for a kind of guitar), *samba de chaula* (a very sexy version), "samba from the upper town", and so on.

At Carnival time, whether in Salvador, Rio or elsewhere, there is a samba for everything. Yet rarely will a samba be heard the same way twice, since the music as well as the dances and costumes are constantly being updated and refurbished, adding new fillips of excitement to the existing formulas.

Though the music of Carnival tends to be a rough and ready kind, it has

always fascinated the cognoscenti among musicians. The classic musicians' account of the Rio Carnival was written by the French composer Darius Milhaud, who visited Rio during the Carnival season of 1917 and "immediately sensed the mood of crazy gaiety that possessed the whole town". One of the favourite amusements of the dancers, he noted, was to improvise words to a repeated tune. "The singer has to keep on finding new words, and as soon as his imagination begins to flag, someone else takes his place."

Milhaud at first found the complexities of the tango rhythms of his day hard to define. "There was an imperceptible pause in the syncopation, a

An agile practitioner of *capoeira*—an acrobatic form of ritual combat devised by African slaves—cartwheels away from an opponent during a bout in Salvador. Movements are accompanied by a man playing a tambourine and two boys plucking *berimbaus*— single-wired, bow-like instruments.

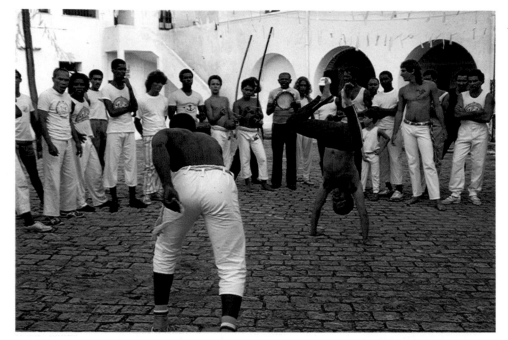

careless catch in the breath, a slight hiatus which I found difficult to grasp," Milhaud wrote. But eventually he learnt the knack of playing the Carnival pieces on the piano—with their syncopated rhythms that ran from one hand to the other—by listening to a popular pianist whose "elusive, mournful, liquid way of playing also gave me deeper insight into the Brazilian soul."

The samba tradition that Milhaud observed continues to this day, changing and developing just as pop music evolved from the sound of Elvis to that of the Beatles and beyond. A major development occurred in the late 1950s with the bossa nova movement. While the classical samba has a strong melodic line, the bossa nova de-emphasizes the tune, so as to integrate it more closely with the other musical parameters—harmony and rhythm.

These days, the samba struggles to maintain its popularity in the face of rock music, and its devotees today are older than those of the 1930s and 40s. But the sound of Brazilian rock has itself been influenced by the samba tradition: one of the musical heroes of modern Brazil, Gilberto Gil, sings rock songs grafted on to the rootstock of Carnival music: "From the city runs electricity in my brain; from the cars run gasolene in my veins . . . I am the electric man. Come and get a shock!"

Whatever the future direction of Brazilian popular music, it is certain to be ubiquitous. Music pulses through every corner of Brazil, taken for granted like the sun. In every bar, someone will be playing the guitar, in every restaurant, a singer performing. On the beach, someone will pick out a rhythm on a drum and in no time it will be echoed up and down the shore by other

sun-worshippers. Even the traveller on a bus finds the whole vehicle rocking rhythmically as, one by one, the passengers take up a popular tune and sway to the beat.

Nothing can drown the Brazilian's love of music, but in the late 20th century they have developed two competing passions: television and football. Brazil now has one of the largest television networks in the world. Three quarters of Brazil's urban households and a fifth of its rural households have television sets. Their favourites are the soap operas of extraordinarily high quality produced in Rio and São Paulo. A number of them have been sold abroad, and foreigners have found themselves becoming almost as addicted to these slices of Brazilian life as are the Brazilians themselves.

Football is Brazil's national obsession and it is no accident that among the country's largest and most impressive buildings are the immense soccer stadiums that can be found in every city worthy of the name. Brazilians are famous for bringing football to new heights of skill, developing an unrivalled repertoire of kicks, dribbles and swerves. Football is more an art form than an act of aggression and the crowd judge the play with the appreciation of connoisseurs.

Though tense with excitement, football matches are invariably good humoured. Some of the spectators wave huge flags, others belt out samba on drums and trumpets. When the player with the ball evades an opponent with a spectacular piece of footwork, no ugly insults are heard from the supporters of the opposition. Instead, as if acknowledging a victorious toreador at a Spanish bullfight, the crowd cry with one voice "*Olé!*"

Passengers aboard a ship on the River
Madeira, a tributary of the Amazon, lie
in colourful hammocks slung above the
deck. Light, portable and ideal for use
in a hot climate, the hammock is the
one Amerindian artefact that has been
readily adopted throughout Brazil.

The white robes of a Carmelite friar highlight the opulent gold and marble ornamentation of the baroque sacristy in Salvador's Convento do Carmo. Founded in 1586, the convent—now a museum—is a monument to the great wealth and power of the Catholic Church in Brazil.

LAND OF MANY GODS

With more than 90 per cent of its 130 million population professing the Roman Catholic faith, Brazil claims to be the world's most Catholic nation. Every town and village has its own patron saint whose festival is marked with processions and public celebrations, and each year millions of the devout go on pilgrimages to the country's holy places. Catholicism is the official state religion, and yet 30 million or more Brazilians exercise their legal right to freedom of belief. Moreover, they see no contradiction between being Catholics and, at the same time, members of one of the mystical sects that originated in Africa or in Brazil itself.

Such heterodoxy owes much to the historical tolerance of Brazilian Catholicism, which has clasped both African religion and Indian beliefs to its embrace and absorbed their spirits and deities into its cosmology. The Church authorities encourage spiritists, such as followers of Macumba and Candomblé, to play an active part in Christian ceremonies and festivals.

Its baroque contours ablaze in the January night, Salvador's Church of Nosso Senhor do Bonfim is lit up for an annual festival combining Catholic and Candomblé elements. Candomblé followers identify Jesus Christ with Oxalá, their supreme god.

Three pilgrims sit impassively at Padre Cicero's birthplace in the village of Crato, some 25 kilometres from his church at Juàzeiro. A bust of the priest stands on the table behind them, protected by a plastic shroud and surrounded by vases of flowers.

A SHRINE TO PADRE CICERO

The village of Juàzeiro do Norte, in the hot, dry province of Ceará, is one of Brazil's foremost places of pilgrimage. Here, in 1889, a priest named Padre Cicero was administering communion to Maria de Araújo when she fell to the ground and the wafer dropped from her lips, covered in blood. Padre Cicero believed this was a miracle, and that the communion wine had turned into Christ's blood, but the Church authorities refused to confirm it. When thousands of believers hastened to Juàzeiro and there were reports of new miracles, the padre was ordered by his superiors to leave the village. But, encouraged by his supporters, Padre Cicero decided instead to break with the Church and declared himself Mayor of Juàzeiro. For two decades he ruled the area, and troops sent to evict him were repulsed. Yet Padre Cicero's faith proved so inspiring that, before he died in 1934, he was reconciled with the Church authorities.

In Juàzeiro's main square, thousands of visitors swarm round a gigantic statue of Padre Cicero. A typical wayside stall *(below)* offers plaster models of the famous priest clutching a bright red prayer book. His effigy stands cheek by jowl with images of the Virgin Mary and other sacred figures.

131

RITUAL OFFERINGS TO A SEA GODDESS

The millions of Brazilian adherents of the gods and spirits of African cults are by no means confined to the descendants of slaves. Initiates come from every class and colour, and many regard the synthesis of African religion and Christianity as Brazil's true national religion. Indeed, African gods have become identified with Christian saints: Yemanjá, goddess of the sea, is linked with the Virgin Mary, while St. George is associated with Ogun, god of war.

In Macumba, as in many other cults, initiates seek possession by the spirits in order to request their assistance or advice. Drumming, chanting and dancing all help to create a trance-like state in which such possession can take place, and the atmosphere of frenzy is heightened by the sacrificing of small animals.

A young woman *(below)* undergoes the first stage of initiation into the Macumba cult, being bathed in the purifying water of the sea. A lock of her hair will be cut off, and during the next three weeks she will learn the elaborate chants and dances of the cult before passing into full membership.

On New Year's Eve, Macumba followers create an impromptu shrine on the beach at Rio de Janeiro and prepare a toy boat as an offering to Yemanjá. At midnight they will launch the boat and carry flowers into the waves, hoping the goddess will grant their wishes during the coming year.

133

SUMMONS TO THE SPIRITS

A Hollywood-style temple at the Valley of the Dawn, a high desert plateau 40 kilometres from Brasília, is the home of a spiritist cult founded in the 1960s by a Brazilian woman mystic named Tia Neiva (Aunt Snow) and her lawyer husband, Mario Sassi. Claiming descent from beings who arrived from a distant planet some 32,000 years ago, they acknowledge the existence of Christ but teach that the world is entering a new era of widespread sickness and anxiety. By dispelling evil spirits from the earth they hope to ease this change and bring comfort and self-fulfilment to the suffering. An endless stream of pilgrims, many of them poor and infirm peasants, visit the temple to witness ceremonies—which are performed by anything up to 3,000 initiates— and to purchase souvenirs, such as portraits of Tia Neiva and bottles of "curing" water.

A cult member shows young pilgrims a statue of White Arrow, the master of the solar system in his incarnation as a 16th-century Bolivian Indian chief who resisted the Spanish conquest. He was so named because his arrows were never red with blood—all his victories were won by peaceful diplomacy.

In an hour-long ceremony, male
initiates dressed in dark heavy robes
prostrate themselves on individual
"tombstones" round a star-shaped
lake, to draw the evil spirits from the
earth. The women, wearing bright
ethereal dresses, can then transmit the
spirits to a safer realm.

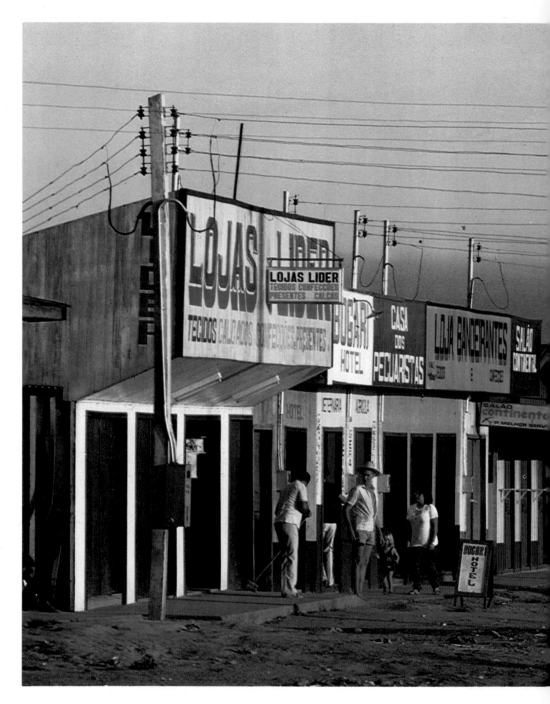

OPENING UP THE LAST FRONTIER

On Christmas Day 1541, a 60-man party of Spaniards, led by a one-eyed conquistador called Francisco de Orellana, set out by boat down the Napo river in Peru to find food for their comrades. They were part of an expedition that had come to South America in search of rare spices and the fabled city of El Dorado, but which was now marooned and starving in the foothills of the Andes. Orellana's group—which included a friar, Gaspar de Carvajal, who kept a record of the voyage—soon found food, but the men had lost the strength or the will to row back up the Napo. So they went on, drifting over 1,400 kilometres downstream until, on February 11, they debouched into another river so large, so powerful, that they believed themselves doomed. "It came on with such fury and with so great an onrush," wrote Carvajal, "that it was enough to fill one with the greatest fear to look at it, let alone to go through it ... and it was so wide from bank to bank from here on that it seemed as though we were navigating launched out upon a vast sea."

Swept along by the mighty currents, the Spaniards followed the river eastwards. Hunger was their main threat. Sometimes they found Indians who were willing to give them food, and sometimes they raided villages to seize provisions by force, but when all other supplies failed, they were reduced to eating their belts and the soles of their shoes boiled with herbs. At last, eight months after leaving their comrades, the Spaniards sailed out of the river's mouth into the Atlantic, having navigated the great waterway for more than 4,000 kilometres.

They made their way up the coast of Venezuela to safety, bringing tales of real and imagined riches, of large cities glistening in white, and of fierce warrior women who, said Carvajal, "were very white and tall and had their hair braided and wrapped round their heads. They were very muscular and wore skins to cover their shameful parts, and with bows and arrows in their hands, they made as much war as ten men." This account was carried back to Spain and so inflamed the imagination of the royal court that they named the river the Amazon, after the warrior women of Greek myth.

The story of the Amazon, which starts with myth, continues with dreams—dreams of finding lost civilizations deep in the interior, dreams of turning "a land without men" into a homeland for "men without land", dreams, above all, of discovering great treasures in the wilderness. Here, in 1933, a 23-year-old gold digger at an open-cast mine found an 80 per cent pure nugget weighing 62.3 kilograms—part of a half-billion-dollar haul unearthed in the first three years of the mine's operation. Here, between 1970 and 1985, over one million poor and dispossessed Brazilians settled to try and carve a new life out of the

The unpaved main street and clapboard buildings testify to the makeshift beginnings of a new pioneer town in the state of Mato Grosso. In the vastness of north-western Brazil, new towns quickly spring up as settlers move in to seek a new life as ranch hands, smallholders or prospectors.

6

wilderness. Here, the dreams of European colonists have made a nightmare for the Amazonian Indians, the main casualties in a centuries-long conflict between modern man and nature.

With an area in excess of four million square kilometres—nearly half the total area of Brazil—Amazonia is vast enough to accommodate the most grandiose of visions. If it were a country, it would rank seventh largest in the world, behind Australia but ahead of India. If all its trees were felled, one third of the world's forest area would have been lost, for Amazonia, as one 19th-century English botanist observed, is "clad with trees and little else but trees ... enormous trees, crowned with magnificent foliage, decked with fantastic parasites, and hung over with lianas, which varied in thickness from slender threads to huge python-like masses."

In shape, Amazonia resembles an ovate leaf, with veins made up of more than a thousand rivers converging on a central rib formed by the Amazon itself. With a length of about 6,000 kilometres, the Amazon is a little shorter than the Nile, but by any other reckoning it is the greatest river in the world. It is estimated that the Amazon and its 1,100 tributaries carry down to the sea one fifth of all the fresh water in the world, discharging it at the rate of about 10 billion litres per second from its mouth. So great is the flow that it pushes back the salt sea water for 160 kilometres offshore—a fact first reported by the man credited with finding the Amazon, the Spanish sea captain Vincente Yáñez Pinzón, who thought he had discovered a freshwater sea until he followed the silt-stained current into the main trunk of the river.

Many of the Amazon's tributaries are mighty in their own right: 17 are more than 1,500 kilometres long, and 10 carry more water than the Mississippi. Ocean-going freighters can penetrate 3,600 kilometres up the main river to Iquitos, their passage assisted by the extremely shallow gradient of the watercourse, which drops less than 100 metres between Iquitos and the sea. In fact, were it not that the Amazon runs close to the equator, the flatness of its basin would ensure that most of Amazonia was permanently flooded and uninhabitable. As it is, the northern and southern tributaries rise in different hemispheres with different rainy seasons, so only about half the rivers are in flood at the same time, which limits the Amazon's annual rise and fall to about 10 metres.

Another startling feature of Amazonia's rivers is their different colours. The Amazon itself, and most of the tributaries flowing from the Andes, are yellowish-white in colour because they are heavily laden with silt; this indicates that the Andes are young mountains from which soil nutrients have not yet been washed. By contrast, the River Negro, which drains from highlands to the north, has black, clear water—indicating that the rocks at its source are so old that they have been leached of their minerals. The contrast is spectacularly evident when the River Negro meets the Amazon near Manaus: the two streams flow side by side for 80 kilometres with a clearly visible boundary between them.

This colour coding provides a simple clue to the geological history of Amazonia. The highlands from which the mineral-deficient waters flow were formed more than 200 million years ago, when the Amazon basin was still part of the super-continent of Gondwanaland, which included Antarctica, South America, Africa, India and Australia. About 140 million years ago, Gondwanaland broke up, and the pieces drifted apart to become the present continents—huge rafts of relatively light granite rocks floating on "plates" of denser basalts.

South America split away from what is now Africa and drifted westwards until it collided with the Nazca Plate, which forms the floor of the south-east Pacific Ocean. The impact crumpled the young rocks at the edge of the South American Plate into giant folds, creating the Andes. The mountains blocked the old mouth of the Amazon, damming the waters in a huge freshwater lake, but some time in the last 50 million years—probably as a result of the continent tilting to the east—the lake burst through the gap between the ancient rocks to north and south, creating the Amazon basin of today.

Three million years ago, further continental movement linked up North and South America at the Isthmus of Panama, providing a land bridge across which plants and animals could migrate in both directions. About the same time, the earth entered the present era of ice ages and interglacials, but Amazonia's position astride the equator meant that it escaped the killing cold, and much of the flora and fauna that evolved during the region's millions of years of isolation has survived to the present day.

Amazonia, in fact, is the most mature woodland on earth—more than 9,000 times older than the forests of North America and Eurasia, which have established themselves only since the last ice age. It is the richest storehouse of genes in the world, with a

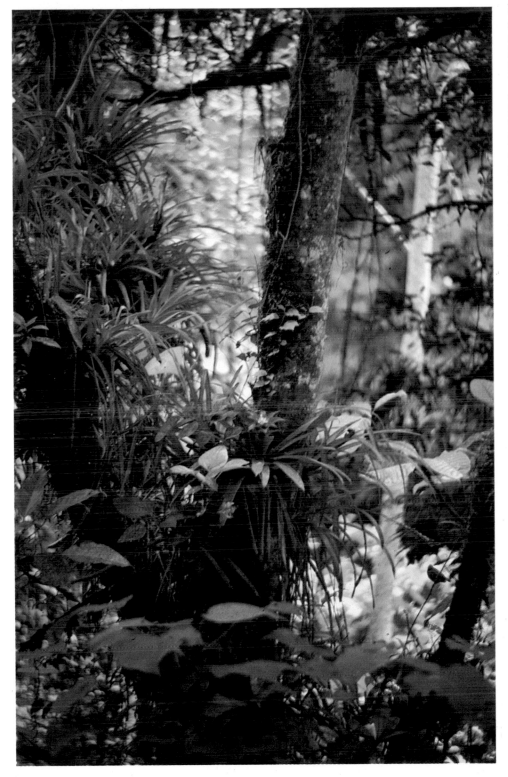

bewildering abundance of animal, insect and plant species, many not yet classified. Something like a tenth of all known species are found in Amazonia, including an estimated 80,000 plants, 1,500 fishes, 200 snakes, and almost one quarter of the world's total of 8,600 bird species. Seven hundred species of butterfly have been collected within an hour's walk of Belém. More than 700 different species of fish—nearly as many as in all North American fresh waters—have been recorded within a 32-kilometre radius of Manaus.

And yet this luxuriant hothouse rests on very poor foundations; it is a trompe l'œil of abundance painted by nature to disguise its basic infertility. Only the 4 per cent of Amazonia which is flooded by the silt-rich rivers of the Andes has truly fecund soils; the rest, leached by aeons of tropical rains, is about as fertile as a brick. Some scientists describe the region as a "desert covered with trees". The Amazon rainforest is an amazing balancing act in which every species plays a mutually dependent part. It is luxuriant because every resource of nature passes through the ecosystem; nothing is wasted. Every scrap of nutrient, every sunbeam, every drop of water is processed in elaborations of chemistry and behaviour that make Amazonia the world's greatest biological laboratory.

In this miracle of mutual adaptation, only the highest trees—ranging from 35 to 45 metres—get the full benefit of the equatorial sunshine. Their fruits and leaves support colonies of monkeys, snakes and birds, which seldom leave the forest canopy. Lower down is a second layer of trees, more tolerant of shade, which grow to heights of between seven and 20 metres and house their own animal denizens.

The leisurely curves of the mighty Amazon river wind eastwards towards the Atlantic Ocean some 335 kilometres away. Fed by 17 major tributaries, the

6,000-kilometre-long Amazon drains an area larger than Europe; huge tracts of the basin are still only partially explored and settled.

6

Scrambling through and over these layers are numerous climbing plants, ferns, orchids, algae and mosses, feeding on each other and at the same time interdependent. The forest floor is gloomy, for only about 10 per cent of the sunlight penetrates this far; and it is strangely uncluttered, because almost everything consumable, even a falling leaf, is recycled into the biomass before it reaches the ground. As a result, the soil is thin and the roots of the trees often penetrate no more than half a metre into the ground. Even the biggest trees rely to a large extent for their support on the lianas which stretch from trunk to trunk.

Into this fragile and complex world came man, between 20,000 and 40,000 years ago, adapting his way of life to fit the contours of nature. Amazonia's Indians, descendants of the Mongoloid Asians who crossed into the Americas via the Bering Straits during the last ice age, traditionally practise a hunter-gatherer economy that makes no serious inroads on the forest's resources.

Traditionally, the 180 or so Amazonian tribes, who speak nearly as many languages and dialects, live in groups seldom larger than 200, in large communal houses with sections for each family to sling its hammocks—an Amerindian invention. Nearby they clear a small patch by slashing and burning the trees and undergrowth. Here they grow manioc, a tuber whose bitter poisons have to be squeezed out before it is edible; but most of their food comes from the forest itself. Fish usually form the meat staple, and the Indians have many different ways of catching them—by netting, trapping, shooting with bows and arrows, paralysing with poisons derived from any of a hundred toxic plants, and luring with lights or special whistles and calls.

Land animals of all sizes are also hunted and eaten—from pig-like capybaras, which are actually rodents, to tiny tree frogs the size of a thumbnail. If game is scarce, the forest provides fruits, nuts and edible grubs for gatherers skilled enough to find them and experienced enough to distinguish the poisonous from the non-poisonous.

Nearly all work is done communally, but is divided between the sexes. The men hunt, defend the tribal territories and build the houses, while the women tend the crops, care for the infants and cook. Political structures are rudimentary and there are no real social divisions within a tribe: even headmen or chiefs have only limited influence. The only person in a community with a specialized role is the shaman—a healer and an intermediary between the tribe and its spirit gods, with whom he speaks in a trance often induced by hallucinatory drugs.

Every 10 years or so, the group abandons its settlement and moves to another part of the rainforest. The decision to leave is usually made collectively by the men, who will consider whether their manioc plots are losing their fertility, whether their houses have got beyond repair, and whether game is becoming scarce. When they go, the forest soon reclaims their land.

Consciously and unconsciously, the Indians keep their populations at a level which is in balance with the availability of resources. Some women take a drink distilled, appropriately, from the passion flower, which appears to stop ovulation the way modern oral contraceptives do. Some tribes, such as the Tapirapé, who live near the Araguaia river in the south-eastern part of Amazonia, practise selective infanticide. Their women are not allowed to have more than three children or more than two of the same sex, and unwanted babies are left to die in the forest. Numbers are also kept stable by intertribal battles which result from territorial rivalry. Among the Yanomami in the north, for example, about a quarter of the male population end their lives violently.

The actual number of Indians living in Amazonia is difficult to estimate because some areas of rainforest are still unexplored and may harbour hitherto unknown tribes—such as the 95-strong group of Arara Indians who were discovered in 1984 in the state of Pará. But even if more tribes are found, it is unlikely that the total population exceeds 200,000—a sad remnant of the two to five million Amerindians who were estimated to inhabit Brazil at the time that Orellana made his epic navigation of the Amazon.

The first objective account of Amazonia's Indians was provided by a Jesuit priest, Father Cristóbal de Acuña, who accompanied a Portuguese expedition that travelled the length of the Amazon between 1637 and 1641. Acuña described how one Indian tribe kept ponds stocked with thousands of turtles near their villages, and how another produced pottery delicate enough to rival Chinese ceramics. But on the return journey he witnessed the savagery with which the Indians were treated by Portuguese slavers from Belém, which had been established in 1616 on the Amazon estuary. He watched in horror as one gang rounded up Indian men while allowing their own Indian auxiliaries to rape the women, and as the expedition neared Belém he found that the whole area

AMAZONIA'S GOLDEN MOUNTAIN

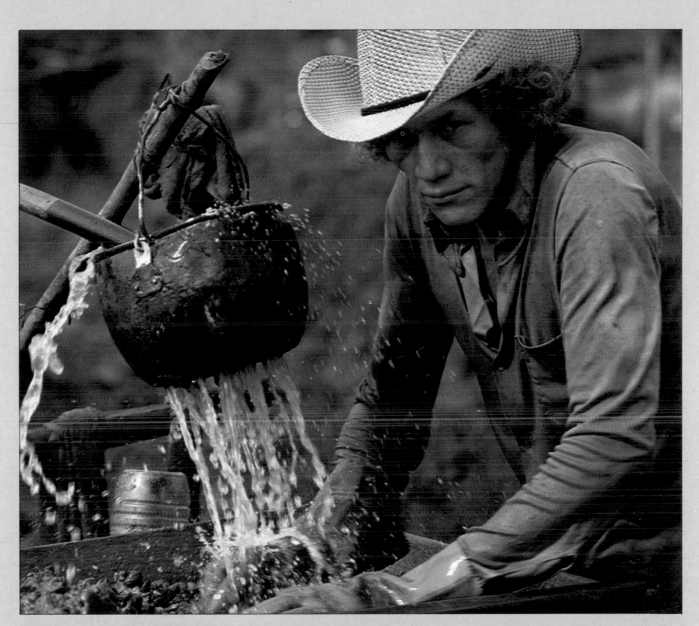

A prospector at the Serra Pelada mine glances up warily as he sluices a box of earth for grains of gold. Some of the makeshift methods used for recovering gold have changed little in centuries. Here, a cooking pot peppered with holes in its base is used to break the force of the water jet from the hose.

In January 1980, a tree on the Serra Pelada, a low mountain some 500 kilometres south of the mouth of the Amazon, blew over in a tropical storm. An amazed rancher, according to one story, discovered several gold nuggets as big as his fist nestling in the tree roots, and so set off a gold rush that within a month brought 10,000 gold-hungry prospectors to the area. Impoverished peasants, illiterates from city slums, as well as lawyers and teachers flooded in to stake claims and tear into the mountainside for the precious metal. The rowdy, gun-toting colony that sprang up had all the *(continued over)*

An army of diggers toil inside the mud-
filled pit which was once the Serra
Pelada mountain. Despite its anarchic
appearance, the mine is divided into
over 1,000 separate claims.

144

Caked with earth, two prospectors *(right)* emerge from the mine carrying sacks of dirt. The rough ladders nearby provide their only means of access to and from the mine 60 metres below.

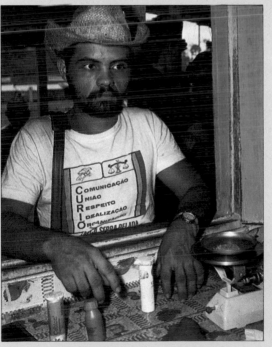

flavour of a Californian gold rush camp of the 1840s, with gambling, prostitution and bitter feuds over shifting claim boundaries.

Five months later the army moved in to bring order. Women and alcohol were banned from the site and claims were set at six square metres per person. Gangs of 20 to 30 miners were hired by each claim owner, usually for a share of the profits, to dig and pan for gold dust. A few miners have become very wealthy men overnight—an estimated $1 billion worth of gold, or more, was extracted in the first four years—but, for the majority of diggers, striking it rich remains a tantalizing dream.

A prospector waits anxiously while his gold dust is weighed by a government official. Before the man is given a receipt for its worth and the money deposited in his account, the gold will be checked with magnets in case it has been adulterated with metal filings.

around the settlement had been denuded of its native population.

The Jesuit missionary Father António Vieira, who arrived in 1653, preached fiery sermons against the slavers. "All of you are in mortal sin; all of you live in a state of condemnation; and all of you are going directly to hell," he thundered. Yet in their desire to "save" the souls of the Indians, the Jesuits directly contributed to their decline by encouraging them to leave the forest for mission villages, where they died in their thousands from European diseases against which they had no resistance. Nor did the Jesuits' denunciation of the slavers stop the slavers exploiting the native labour.

The real wealth of Amazonia was discovered by European naturalists, who began arriving in the region in the mid-18th century. To them, the rivers and their companion rainforests were a cornucopia of scientific marvels. One of the first and most important was the brilliant French polymath Charles Marie de la Condamine, mathematician, map-maker, astronomer and naturalist. He arrived in Brazil in 1743 and mapped the Amazon with remarkable accuracy. While studying its flora and fauna, he also investigated some of the poisons used by the Indians on their arrows and blowgun darts, and how they fished by beating the surface of the stream with certain creepers that left a chemical in the water to stun the fish. From the cinchona tree, he collected seeds which the Indians used as a prophylactic for malaria; the drug later came to be known as quinine. From the tree which the Indians called "the wood that weeps" he collected a milky sap that amazed him by its elasticity. He took samples of it back to Paris, but it was more than a hundred years before the invention of the motor car created a huge demand for latex.

La Condamine was followed in 1800 by the German naturalist and explorer Friedrich von Humboldt, who investigated native poisons and tested the voltage generated by electric eels, after he had stepped on one of these brutes and received a shock that affected him for a day "with a violent pain in the knees and in almost every joint".

The most complete and valuable studies of Amazonia's natural history were made by two self-taught English scientists, Henry Walter Bates, a former hosier's apprentice, and Alfred Russel Wallace, who started his career as a surveyor's assistant. They met by chance in Leicester and, finding that they shared a fascination for the Amazon, they sailed for Belém in 1848, hoping to support themselves by sending plant and animal specimens to the British Museum and the Royal Botanic Gardens at Kew at threepence apiece. For reasons that were not disclosed, they went their own ways soon after they reached South America, although they remained lifelong friends.

Bates spent 11 years in Amazonia, amassing a collection of 14,712 species, of which 8,000 were new to science— including bird-eating spiders as big as a fist. "One day," he recorded in his vivid and delightful *The Naturalist on the River Amazons*, "I saw the children belonging to an Indian family who collected for me with one of these monsters secured by a cord round its waist, by which they were leading it about the house as they would a dog."

Wallace's expedition lasted for four years and his studies of the distribution and divergence of rainforest species planted the seeds of a theory about evolution by natural selection which closely paralleled Charles Darwin's epoch-making work. In 1858 both men delivered papers to the Linnean Society in London, and although Darwin was credited with the discovery of the laws of evolution, Wallace never displayed any resentment, telling his old friend Bates: "I could never have approached the completeness of his work."

But many explorers sensationalized their accounts of Amazonia, describing it as a "green hell", a "wilderness of fools" or a "lost world" swarming with man-eating snakes, bloodthirsty headhunters and lustful Indian women. One of the more scholarly of these travellers was ex-President of the United States Theodore Roosevelt, who made an expedition in Mato Grosso, where a river he discovered still bears his name. Amazonia, he enthused, was the "world's last true frontier".

Just before World War I, when Roosevelt was adventuring in Amazonia, most of the vast region was, indeed, unknown to any besides the Amerindians who lived there, and remained almost completely untouched by the industrial world. Even the rubber boom, which had lasted a scant 30 years and had swollen the population of Amazonia by 90,000, had not seriously encroached on the forest. No roads had been built, for the raw material was transported by steamers down the river; no plantations had been cleared, for the industry depended on tapping the sap of trees which grew wild in the forest. Even the extravagant city of Manaus, built by the rubber barons, had reverted to an isolated outpost.

An attempt to revive the rubber industry was made in 1924 when the state of Pará gave Henry Ford one million hectares to establish a rubber plantation. He planned to regain Brazil's old position as the world's leading rubber producer, but his trees, planted in neat lines and tended by workers lodged in a new town called Fordlandia, lacked the protection they had in their natural state and were highly vulnerable to disease and pests. In 1946 Ford pulled out and sold the project to the Brazilian government for $250,000. The company's investment had been more than $30 million.

So, once again the vision of an eldorado had disappeared into the green vastness. The rainforest was left to a few immigrant rubber tappers stranded after the collapse of the rubber industry, and to a trickle of landless peasants from the backlands of the north-east hoping to find some sort of living in Amazonia. To these people, the Indians were a mortal foe and

treated accordingly. Small as the new settlers' numbers were, the Indians, armed only with bows and arrows, were beginning to be driven from their traditional hunting grounds.

The first major initiative to protect the natives was undertaken at the turn of the century by a young army officer called Cândido Mariano da Silva Rondon. He was given the job of mapping parts of the wilderness and establishing telegraphic links between settlements, but in the course of his travels he met several isolated Indian tribes and grew to appreciate their culture. In 1910 he persuaded the government to set up the SPI, the Service for the Protection of Indians.

· Appalled by the brutality with which the encroaching settlers treated the native population, Rondon set himself the task of creating a society in which whites and Indians would co-

exist peacefully, with Indians being given their own land until they could be assimilated into Brazilian society. First he had to establish friendly contact with the forest-dwellers, and he did this by sending assistants to leave gifts such as axes, cooking pots and mirrors near Indian settlements. It was dangerous work, demanding considerable self-sacrifice, for Rondon strictly enforced his slogan: "Die if necessary, but do not kill."

His efforts were recognized worldwide; in Brazil he was promoted to the rank of marshal and the Amazonian federal territory of Rondônia was named after him. But after his death in 1958 the SPI became corrupt, and a decade later it was disbanded after a commission of enquiry found that it had collaborated with land speculators in the massacre of entire tribes by bombing and machine-gunning, the

6

use of poisoned sweets to kill infants and the deliberate spreading of disease through presents of infected clothing.

Claudio Villas Boas, one of three brothers who continued Rondon's work through a new agency, FUNAI, the National Indian Foundation, delivered a sad epitaph on his mentor's work: "He ended his long and noble life in 1958, covered in glory, without realizing that all his work on behalf of the Indians had been turned against them. He had given them land: it was the signature of their death sentence... Once the Indians were tamed by a man of noble spirit, they were then defenceless in the face of adventurers who arrived hotfoot after him."

Large-scale encroachment of the Amazon rainforest by land speculators, cattle ranchers and land-hungry peasants started in the early 1960s following the construction of the Belém to Brasília road, "the spine of Brazil". The human influx was given fresh impetus in 1966 by the new military administration when it launched "Operation Amazonia", an ambitious plan to promote settlement in the region and integrate it fully into the economy. SUDAM, the Superintendency for the Development of the Amazon, was the state agency for this plan, which was built around generous tax incentives for investors. The scheme was very attractive to businessmen, who bought large tracts of land for ranching or land speculation. But it also attracted some foreigners, like the American entrepreneur Daniel K. Ludwig, whose ill-fated Jari project was intended to capture a major slice of the world market in wood pulp.

Underpinning "Operation Amazonia" was a massive programme of road building, which was pushed through at breakneck speed. In 1970 there were only 1,530 kilometres of rough roads and 270 kilometres of paved roads in the whole of Amazonia. By the end of 1976 the network had been expanded to 15,000 kilometres of dirt roads and 2,600 kilometres of paved highway—one third of this total made up by the Trans-Amazonian Highway, which stretches 5,600 kilometres from João Pessoa on the Atlantic coast to the Peruvian frontier in the west.

The new roads particularly helped cattle ranchers by making large-scale transport of livestock to market economically viable. From 1966 to 1978 SUDAM gave the go-ahead to 358 ranches, for which it authorized tax rebates of $750 million. But many beneficiaries of this largesse had no intention of using their land for cattle ranching, seeing their spreads as little more than a property investment obtained at a give-away price. Of the 358 projects approved by SUDAM, it is estimated that only about a hundred actually got off the ground, and few of these were successful.

Most of the ranchers knew little about tropical farming and made the mistake of assuming the rainforest soil was fertile. Some cleared the land by the traditional "slash-and-burn" method; some used a 100-metre chain slung between gigantic tractors to topple all the trees in its path; others sprayed defoliants from aircraft. In the first 10 years, nearly 120,000 square kilometres of forest were cleared, and most of this was intensively stocked with cattle. But with the protective canopy removed, the soil became impoverished within two or three years, and the ranchers' dream withered among weed growth and soil erosion.

148

A gigantic wood-pulp mill sprawls incongruously in the midst of primeval forest on the banks of the Jari river. Floated complete all the way from Japan in 1978, the plant was only part of a massive scheme to exploit Amazonia's resources, which included mining and cattle ranching.

6

Some ranches only lasted two years; others held out for as long as seven. One rancher, who bought 40,000 hectares in north Pará, summed up the problems of farming in Amazonia: "It's like a marriage," he admitted ruefully. "It all goes well the first year or two, but then the problems begin."

By 1976 the failure of the cattlemen could no longer be ignored by the government, and in 1979 tax rebates for new ranches in the rainforest were discontinued. Attention now turned to the state of Rondônia on the southern fringe of the Amazonian rainforest, which was considered suitable for settlement of Brazil's 10 million-strong army of landless peasants. A few individuals had started arriving in the area during the 1970s with the construction of the new roads, but after 1976, when the government promised the distribution of one million free land titles in Rondônia, the trickle became a flood. In 1977, in one border post, 275 immigrants passed through a government processing centre; in 1983 the number was 430,265.

The colonists were given 8 to 16-hectare plots, laid out in a grid pattern that paid scant regard to the quality of soil or availability of water on individual holdings. Many of the plots proved to be unfarmable, and a large proportion of the colonists, exhausted by fruitless toil and tempted by cash offers for their land, sold out. Even so, the flood of migrants continued. Many spent up to four years on waiting lists for their allotments of land, eking out a living by working as casual labourers for ranchers or established farmers.

To service the influx of settlers, new towns have sprung up almost overnight; Rolim de Moura, for example, which was founded in 1978, had a population of 60,000 by 1985. Such towns look and behave very like the frontier towns of the American Old West as portrayed by Hollywood. Farm labourers, horseless equivalents of the cowboys, often work 12-hour days for three-month contract periods, without women or drink, and when they reach town they vent their frustration in wild and frequently violent orgies in the bars and brothels.

Another similarity with the Wild West is the conflict between the cattlemen and squatters. Some of the ranch owners buy their land without having seen it, and when they make their first visit they arrive to find it already occupied by peasants who, under Brazilian law, cannot be evicted without compensation if they have lived on their plots for a year and a day. If the peasants have been living and farming in one place for over 10 years without any contact with a landowner, the property becomes theirs.

But on this frontier the law is not always observed, and dark tales are told of the pro-rancher bias of land apportionment officials and the corruption of the police and courts. Some ranchers, having failed to persuade peasants to leave their land, hire gunmen to eject them by force. Many peasant families have been illegally evicted from plots three or four times, but cannot afford to contest their cases in court. In 1975, however, the Catholic Church established a national pastoral land commission, the *Commissão Pastoral de Terra* (CPT), to advise and assist the rural poor in standing up for their rights in land disputes. Headed by a number of radical priests, the CPT encouraged families to hold out on their plots, even if threatened by gunmen. In the 1980s, imbued with a new sense of defiance, peasants banded together against the ranchers' hired thugs, which resulted in several fierce and fatal gunfights.

Gold prospectors are another violent element in Amazonia. Attracted to the region for centuries, they have come in vastly increased numbers since gold was discovered at Serra Pelada in 1980. Within a week of the first nugget being unearthed, 1,000 miners were on the site; within a month there were 10,000, and by 1984 there were 40,000 at work in a pit big enough to swallow one of the great pyramids. All work is done by hand, but since few claim owners can afford a large payroll, wages are paid in terms of percentage of the value of a strike—1 per cent for a spoil carrier perhaps, and 2 per cent for a digger, with the terms sometimes written on a cigarette packet or in the margin of a pornographic magazine.

On the River Madeira, on Brazil's Bolivian border, another 4,000 men are trying to get a share of the $300 million of alluvial gold brought up from the river bed each year. The gold is recovered using rafts and what are, in effect, huge vacuum cleaners worked by divers. It is dangerous work: the divers work six-hour shifts, often competing with rival teams poaching on their territory. Down there in the darkness, it is easy for air lines to become entangled, and just as easy for a resentful colleague to cut a lifeline. Officially, 20 divers died in 1984; the actual toll was much higher.

Of the estimated 250,000 prospectors chasing dreams in Amazonia, many operate in small teams in remote areas which are occupied only by forest Indians. These men go heavily armed against surprise attack and tend to regard any Indian they might encounter as an enemy to be shot on sight.

Among ranks of recent graves, mourners in the state of Rondônia wait while a richly decorated coffin is sealed before being lowered into the ground. Untimely death is common in Brazil's frontier regions, where land disputes are often settled by gunfights.

Less destructive of human life, but potentially more damaging to the environment, are the large Brazilian and multinational mining companies that the government has been encouraging into Amazonia to exploit its massive mineral wealth; bauxite, iron ore, tin, manganese and diamonds are just a few of its underground resources. Bauxite mining and aluminium smelting started on a large scale in the early 1980s, and they were soon followed by the even larger Carajás mining project in the state of Pará, to the west of the Araguaia river, which contains the largest reserves of high-grade iron ore in the world.

To exploit the iron ore of Carajás, which also contains huge deposits of other minerals, Brazil has built the $3 billion Tucurui Dam, which will eventually flood 2,200 square kilometres of forest—and engulf the homeland of the Parakana Indians, one group of whom were only discovered in 1976. Until the 1970s the whole tribe had numbered 700 to 1,000, living in three groups, but in 10 years contact with alien diseases had reduced their numbers drastically, to about 300.

Since 1968, when the discredited SPI was replaced as the Indian protection agency by FUNAI, the Brazilian government has set aside large areas of Amazonia to shield the native population from settlers and developers. In 1980, FUNAI supervised four main parks—the Xingu and Aripuaña in Mato Grosso, the Araguaia in Goiás and the Tumucumaque in Pará—and 17 reservations, the combined area of these preserves exceeding 95,000 square kilometres. But, despite this practical demonstration of concern for the Indians, FUNAI is often criticized for its contradictory roles—to preserve the life and culture of the Indians on the one hand, to integrate them into modern society on the other.

Some Indians who live in the parks and reserves have already been compromised by European civilization. The once war-like Kayapo tribe, for example, who live in the Gorotire Reserve on the banks of the River Xingu, have given up their bows and clubs, and their new symbols of manhood are hunting rifles and transistor radios. Young men now wear shorts instead of

With its cub on its back, the lumbering giant anteater is easy prey for pet hunters.

A giant otter surfaces in a pool of dark water.

A three-toed sloth, which has no single relative in the animal kingdom, reaches out to grasp a meal of leaves.

Two capybaras wallow in water. Expert swimmers, they often grow over one metre long.

A giant armadillo, which can reach 60 kilograms in weight, forages for food.

A jaguar lazes in a tree, but it is equally at home in water and often catches fish.

RARE BREEDS IN A THREATENED WORLD

For billions of years the Amazon rainforest has provided a stable environment in which plant and animal life have evolved in thousands of unique forms. But the forest ecosystem is so finely balanced that many species are interdependent, and the loss of one can lead to the loss of another.

Man barely disturbed this balance until the 1960s, when an accelerated programme of dam and road-building, and forest clearance for ranches and mining, made such serious inroads on the habitat of many animals as to threaten them with extinction. The arboreal sloth, for example, cannot easily cross new roads and so is cut off from some of its habitual grazing grounds. This, in turn, deprives plants and insects that depend for survival on the nutrients in the recycled foliage provided by the sloth.

Other species are threatened by hunters after their meat: capybaras, amphibious vegetarians that are the world's largest rodents, are widely eaten, and the giant armadillo is considered a delicacy by Indians. Jaguars and the giant otter are hunted for their fur and for sport, and the latter, once seen in many Brazilian rivers, is now found only in inaccessible parts of Amazonia. Many creatures, such as monkeys, exotic birds and even the giant anteater, have been reduced to pitifully small numbers by man's insatiable desire for curious pets.

Brazil now has laws to protect endangered animals, but the law is almost impossible to enforce in the 3.6 million square kilometres of the rainforest. Scientists fear that some species of both animal and plant life will never again achieve a healthy population size, and will die out—with incalculable loss to mankind.

6

penis sheaths and have abandoned their traditional lip-discs because "you can't speak Portuguese when you are wearing one". The reserve now has churches, schools, mission houses and mobile health teams.

In any case, the parks and reserves may not be able to hold out against economic interests. When uranium was found on the Yanomamo Reserve in Roraima State, the Governor made his position clear: "I am of the opinion that an area as rich as this—with gold, diamonds and uranium—cannot afford the luxury of conserving a half-dozen Indian tribes who are holding back the development of Brazil."

Against pressures like these, the Indians are beginning to fight back, using the white man's own political weapons. Their lead came from CIMI, the Catholic Church's body for Indian affairs, which was radicalized in the early 1970s by the charismatic bishop of São Félix, Dom Pedro Casaldáliga, who helped Indians set up regional, then national, assemblies where they could air concerns and grievances.

Frustrated, however, by what they regard as the government's reluctance to heed their demands, some Indians have used their new-found political sophistication in conjunction with direct-action tactics. For example, in April 1984, a group of Txukarramrae Indians near the Xingu river became exasperated with the government's delay in making out a promised buffer zone to protect their land from encroaching cattle ranches. In a dramatic move, they kidnapped three government officials and threatened to kill them if the zone was not demarcated at once. The government, fearful of the political repercussions if the hostages were to die, rapidly agreed to the demands.

This incident made international headlines, but by then media attention was focusing on a more general concern—the destruction of the rainforest itself and the possible consequences for the global environment. The forest not only protects the soil against erosion, but also manufactures its own rain: research has shown that moisture from leaves—either evaporated from them or released by transpiration—accounts for more than half the rainfall in Amazonia. This leads scientists to fear that a desert the size of Europe would be created if the region were to lose a lot of its tree cover.

There are fears, too, that deforestation could lead to a disastrous global warming by increasing the amount of atmospheric carbon dioxide, a heat trap that constitutes only 0.03 per cent of the volume of the atmosphere but which absorbs 15 per cent of the energy radiated by the earth. According to the most pessimistic forecasters, so much carbon dioxide would be released by burn-off and bacterial activity in the disturbed soil that temperatures would climb high enough to melt the polar ice caps, thus raising the sea level by about 60 metres and flooding many of the world's major cities.

How much of Amazonia has already been destroyed is open to dispute. Apologists claim clearance is a mere 3 per cent of the total, while others say the figure is much greater and that the sensitive balance of the ecosystem has already been damaged beyond recall. These critics question why the forest needs to be disturbed at all. They point out that there is enough cultivable land outside Amazonia to give each Brazilian one hectare—more land than is available in the U.S. They point out that, despite the money poured into

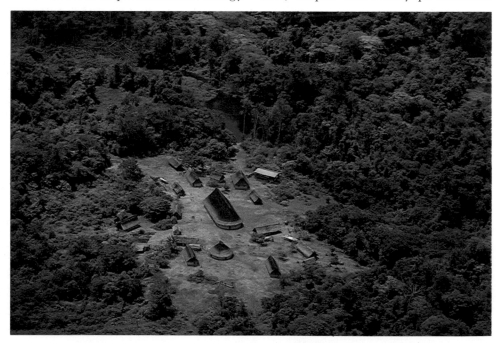

A clearing breaches the forest canopy *(above)*, where Amazonian Indians have erected a thatched *maloca*—a communal house for several families; in a nearby river, four girls kneel in a cloud of butterflies *(right)*. Despite such idyllic scenes, contact with outsiders threatens their way of life.

the settlement of Amazonia, estimated at $12,000 per settler, the region still has only 4 per cent of Brazil's population and produces only 2 per cent of the country's gross national product.

It would be unrealistic, however, to imagine that Amazonia could simply be handed back to nature, but the conservationists believe that it could be exploited in a much more thoughtful way rather than ravished for purely short-term economic and political gain. The billions that were spent on a project like Jari, for example, would have been better spent on developing sustainable methods of culling native hardwoods, for which world demand is high. The Amazon's huge stocks of fish could be a far more valuable source of protein than the expensively introduced cattle which, fed on poor scrub, are fit only for hamburger meat.

Ecologists are concerned that Amazonia is being destroyed before we can find out what other valuable resources it has to offer. It would take scientists decades to evaluate the potential uses of its 80,000 plant species, but according to Richard Schultes, a Harvard botanist who spent 13 years in Amazonia, the Indians, who use more than 1,000 native plants for medicinal and other purposes, may be the shortcut to unlocking the forest's secrets.

Already, Indian lore has given us *curare*, from the *Chondodendron* and *Strychnos* plant species, which Indians use to paralyse game and Western doctors use as a muscle relaxant for heart disease victims, and *rotenone*, from the bark of two plants, used by Indians to paralyse fish and which the industrial world employs as a safe, biodegradable insecticide. Schultes also believes that plants used by the Indians as hallucinogens may be valuable tools in psychiatry, and he has found a species of Amazonian palm that yields a high quality edible oil almost indistinguishable from olive oil. The fact that of the 3,000 plants identified as having anticancer properties, 70 per cent are rainforest species, suggests that Amazonia may yield a cure for one of the world's greatest killers.

Amazonia, in short, still has many treasures to give up—treasures that are potentially of far greater value to man than the El Dorado of the early explorers' dreams.

ACKNOWLEDGEMENTS

The index for this book was prepared by Vicki Robinson. For their help in the preparation of this volume, the editors wish to thank: Antonio Barros, Salvador, Brazil; Brazilian Embassy Information Department, London; Mike Brown, London; Kate Cann, Guildford, Surrey, England; Canning House Library, London; Eduardo Castanho, São Paulo, Brazil; Windsor Chorlton, London; Nina Coelho, Salvador, Brazil; John Cottrell, Weybridge, Surrey, England; Jane Curry, London; Martha de la Cal, Lisbon; De Simoni Associados, São Paulo, Brazil; José Luiz Barcellos Dias, Rio de Janeiro; João Romeu Dutra, Porto Alegre, Brazil; Lito Sarmento Filho, Bagé, Brazil; John Gaisford, London; Helen Grubin, London; Caroline Hill, London; Institute of Latin American Studies, London; Michael Kepp, Rio de Janeiro; João Lacerda, Bagé, Brazil; Vivaldo Costa Lima, Salvador, Brazil; Fred Monteiro, Salvador, Brazil; Salvador Monteiro, Rio de Janeiro; Tony and Marion Morrison, Woodbridge, Suffolk, England; Museu Costa Pinto, Salvador, Brazil; Museu de Arte Sacra, Salvador, Brazil; Robin Olson, London; Maria de Lourdes Noronha Pinto, Porto Alegre, Brazil; Sally Rowland, Saffron Walden, Essex, England; Antonio C. dos Santos-Vovô, Salvador, Brazil; Roberto Stern, Rio de Janeiro; Roberto M. Suñe, Bagé, Brazil; Deborah Thompson, London; Lynn Underwood, London; Varig Brazilian Airlines, London; Edgar Wallau, Porto Alegre, Brazil; Marlene Webber, Library of the Brazilian Embassy, London.

PICTURE CREDITS

Credits from left to right are separated by semicolons, from top to bottom by dashes.

Cover: J. Alex Langley from Aspect Picture Library, London. Front endpaper: Map by Roger Stewart, London. Back endpaper: Digitized image by Ralph Scott/Chapman Bounford, London.

1, 2: © Flag Research Center, Winchester, Massachusetts. **6, 7**: Gerd Ludwig from Visum, Hamburg. **8**: Digitized image by Ralph Scott/Chapman Bounford, London. **8, 9**: Claus C. Meyer from Colorific!, London. **10–13**: Loren McIntyre, Arlington, Virginia, U.S.A. **14**: Martin Rogers from Woodfin Camp Inc., Washington D.C. **15**: Digitized image by Ralph Scott/Chapman Bounford, London. **16, 17**: Claus C. Meyer from Colorific!, London. **18**: Cavan McCarthy from The Hutchison Library, London. **19**: Digitized image by Ralph Scott/Chapman Bounford, London. **20, 21**: Tony Morrison, Woodbridge, Suffolk, England. **22, 23**: Claus C. Meyer from Colorific!, London. **25–29**: Vautier-de-Nanxe, Paris. **30, 31**: Claus C. Meyer from Colorific!, London. **32**: Loren McIntyre, Arlington, Virginia, U.S.A. **34, 35**: Claus C. Meyer from Colorific!, London. **36, 37**: Rodolpho Machado from Colorific!, London. **38, 39**: Claus C. Meyer from Colorific!, London. **40–41**: The Financial Times/Robert Harding Picture Library, London. **42**: Courtesy of the Bibliothèque Nationale, Paris. **44**: Courtesy of the Collection of the Arquivo Historico Ultramarino, Lisbon. **47**: Lithograph by Isidore Laurent Deroy from a watercolour by Johann Rugendas, Museu Raymundo Ottoni de Castro Maia, Rio de Janeiro, courtesy of Fundação Nacional Pró-Memória. **48**: *Soldados Indios de Mogi das Cruzes*, lithograph from a watercolour by Jean-Baptiste Debret, Museu Raymundo Ottoni de Castro Maia, Rio de Janeiro, courtesy of Fundação Nacional Pró-Memória. **50, 51**: Courtesy of the Museu Paulista, Universidade de São Paulo. **53**: Courtesy of the British Museum (Natural History), London. **54**: Medallion from the cloisters of the Jeronimos Church, Lisbon; *Vista de Aqueduto de Santa Teresa*, oil painting by Joaquim Leandro, courtesy of the Museu Nacional de Belas Artes, Rio de Janeiro-*Funcionario do Governo Saindo a Passeio* by Jean-Baptiste Debret, Museu Raymundo Ottoni de Castro Maia, Rio de Janeiro, courtesy of Fundação Nacional Pró-Memória. **55**: BBC Hulton Picture Library, London; *Week of Modern Art*, exhibition catalogue cover by Di Cavalcanti, 1922, courtesy of the Biblioteca Nacional, Rio de Janeiro—The Photo Source, London. **57**: The Burton Holmes Collection, Los Angeles, California, U.S.A. **58**: Photo Maia from Foto Flash, Fortaleza, courtesy of the Museu Historico e Antoropologica do Ceará, Fortaleza, Ceará, Brazil; Film still from *Memória do Cangaço*, dir. Paulo Gil Soares, Cinemateca do M.A.M., Rio de Janeiro. **60, 61**: John Moss from Colorific!, London. **62, 63**: Homer Sykes, London. **64**: Claus C. Meyer from Colorific!, London. **66**: Sarah Errington from the Hutchison Library, London. **67**: Vautier-de-Nanxe, Paris. **68**: Nicholas Devore from Bruce Coleman Ltd., Uxbridge, Middlesex, England; Nobu Arakawa from The Image Bank, London; Sarah Errington from The Hutchison Library, London. **69**: Fred Grunfeld, Mallorca; Jesco Von Puttkamer from The Hutchison Library, London; Tony Morrison, Woodbridge, Suffolk, England. **70**: Loren McIntyre, Arlington, Virginia, U.S.A. **71**: Michael Boys from Susan Griggs Picture Agency, London. **72**: Claus C. Meyer from Black Star/Colorific!, London. **73**: Antonio Gusmão from Colorific!, London. **74, 75**: Dr. Nigel Smith from The Hutchison Library, London. **77**: Vautier-de-Nanxe, Paris. **78–85**: Claus C. Meyer from Colorific!, London. **86, 87**: Loren McIntyre, Arlington, Virginia, U.S.A. **89**: Antonio Gusmão from Colorific!, London. **91**: Claus C. Meyer from Colorific!, London. **92**: Loren McIntyre, Arlington, Virginia, U.S.A. **94**: Tony Morrison, Woodbridge, Suffolk, England. **95**: Gerd Ludwig from Visum, Hamburg—Homer Sykes, London. **97**: Vautier-de-Nanxe, Paris. **98, 99**: Richard House from The Hutchison Library, London. **101**: Vautier-de-Nanxe, Paris. **103**: Claus C. Meyer, from Colorific!, London. **104–111**: Vautier-de-Nanxe, Paris. **112, 113**: Claus C. Meyer from Colorific!, London. **114**: Vautier-de-Nanxe, Paris. **115**: Tony Morrison, Woodbridge, Suffolk, England. **116**: Luiz Claudio Marigo from Bruce Coleman Ltd., Uxbridge, Middlesex, England. **117**: Vautier-de-Nanxe, Paris. **118**: Fred Grunfeld, Mallorca. **119**: The Kobal Collection, London. **120**: Tony Morrison, Woodbridge, Suffolk, England. **122**: *Café*, an oil painting, by Cândido Portinari, 1935, courtesy of the Museu Nacional De Belas Artes, Rio de Janeiro. **123**: John Lewis Stage from The Image Bank, London. **124–126**: Claus C. Meyer from Colorific!, London. **127**: Michael Lange from Visum, Hamburg. **128**: Claus C. Meyer, from Colorific!, London. **129**: J. Alex Langley from Aspect Picture Library, London. **130, 131**: Vautier-de-Nanxe, Paris. **132**: Sebastian Barbosa from The Image Bank, London. **134, 135**: Vautier-de-Nanxe, Paris. **136, 137**: Michael Lange from Visum, Hamburg. **139–141**: Loren McIntyre, Arlington, Virginia, U.S.A. **143–145**: Vautier-de-Nanxe, Paris. **147**: Loren McIntyre, Arlington, Virginia, U.S.A. **148, 149**: Martin Rogers from Woodfin Camp Inc., Washington D.C. **151**: Claus C. Meyer, from Colorific!, London. **152**: Alan Root from Survival Anglia Ltd., London; Keith and Liz Laidler from Survival Anglia Ltd., London (2). **153**: Konrad Wother from Bruce Coleman Ltd., Uxbridge, Middlesex, England—Alan Root from Bruce Coleman Ltd., Uxbridge, Middlesex, England—Loren McIntyre, Arlington, Virginia, U.S.A. **154**: T. Aramac from Colorific!, London. **155**: Loren McIntyre, Arlington, Virginia, U.S.A.

BIBLIOGRAPHY
BOOKS

Amado, Jorge, trans. J. L. Taylor and W. L. Grossman, *Gabriela, Clove and Cinnamon*. Chatto & Windus, London, 1963.

Amado, Jorge, Niemeyer, Oscar, and others, *Brazil*. Thames and Hudson, London, 1971.

Andrade, Geraldo Edson de, *As Festas Brasileiras de los Pintores Populares*, Imprinta, Rio de Janeiro, 1980.

Ayala, Walmir, *O Brasil por Seus Artistas*. Editora Nordica Ltda., Rio de Janeiro (undated).

Azevedo, Fernando de, trans. William Rex Crawford, *Brazilian Culture*. Macmillan, New York, 1950.

Barbican Art Gallery, *Portraits of a Country*. Catalogue of Pictures from the Gilberto Chateaubriand Collection, 1984.

Bastide, Roger, *Les Religions Africaines au Brésil*. Presses Universitaires de France, Paris, 1960.

Bello, José Maria, trans. J. L. Taylor, *A History of*

Modern Brazil, 1886–1950. Stanford University Press, Stanford, 1966.

Bethell, Leslie, *The Abolition of the Brazilian Slave Trade*. Cambridge University Press, Cambridge, 1970.

Bethell, Leslie, ed., *The Cambridge History of Latin America, Volume 11*. Cambridge University Press, Cambridge, 1984.

Botting, Douglas, *Rio de Janeiro* (The Great Cities Series). Time-Life International, Amsterdam, 1977.

Bourne, Richard, *Assault on the Amazon*. Gollancz, London, 1978.

Bourne, Richard, *Getúlio Vargas of Brazil*. Knight & Co., London & Tonbridge, 1974.

Boxer, C. R., *The Golden Age of Brazil*. The University of California, Berkeley, 1962.

Braddon, Russell, Dowell, Christina, Greer, Germaine, and others, *River Journeys*. B.B.C., London, 1984.

Bradford Burns, E., *History of Brazil*. Columbia University Press, New York & London, 1980.

Brazilian Embassy, *Brazil: a Geography*. London, 1984.

Brooks, John, ed., *The South American Handbook 1983*. Trade & Travel Publications, Bath, 1983.

Calva, Ralph della, *Miracle at Joaseiro*. Columbia University Press, New York & London, 1970.

Carmichael, Elizabeth, and Hugh-Jones, Stephen, *The Hidden People of the Amazon*. British Museum, London, 1985.

Carneiro, Edison, and others, *O Negro Brasileiro*. Cadernos Brasileiros, Rio de Janeiro, 1968.

Chandler, Billy Jaynes, *The Bandit King: Lampião of Brazil*. Texas A & M University Press, College Station & London, 1978.

Conrad, John Edgar, *Children of God's Fire*. Princeton University Press, Princeton, 1983.

Cruz, Davidoff, *Divida Externa, e Politica Economica*. Brasiliense, São Paulo, 1984.

Cunha, Euclides da, trans. Samuel Putnam, *Rebellion in the Backlands (Os Sertões)*. Chicago University Press, Chicago & London, 1944.

Degler, Carl, *Neither Black nor White*. Macmillan, New York, 1971.

Dickenson, J. P., *Brazil*. Longman, London, 1982.

Dorst, Jean, *South America: a Natural History*. Hamish Hamilton, London, 1967.

Dulles, John W. F., *Unrest In Brazil*. University of Texas Press, Austin & London, 1970.

Dzidzienyo, Anani, and Casal, Lourdes, *The Position of Blacks in Brazilian and Cuban Society*. Minority Rights Group, London, 1979.

Fernandes, Florestan, *The Negro in Brazilian Society*. Columbia University Press, New York, 1969.

Flynn, Peter, *Brazil: a Political Analysis*. Ernest Benn, London, 1978.

Fodor's Brazil, New York, 1985.

Frater, Alexander, ed., *Great Rivers of the World*. Hodder & Stoughton, London, 1984.

Freyre, Gilberto, trans. Harriet de Onís, *The Mansions and the Shanties (Sobrados e Mucambos)*. Alfred A. Knopf, New York, 1963.

Freyre, Gilberto, trans. Samuel Putnam, *The Masters and the Slaves (Casa-Grande e Senzala)*. Alfred A. Knopf, New York, 1956.

Fundação Bienal de São Paulo, *Tradição e Ruptura*. São Paulo, 1984.

Fundação Getúlio Vargas, *Contas Nacionais, Annuario Estatistico do Brasil*. Rio de Janeiro, 1984.

Furtado, Celso, *Formação Economico do Brasil*. Editora Nacional, Brasília, 1984.

Goodland, R. J. A., and Irwin, H. S., *Amazon Jungle: Green Hell or Red Desert?* Elsevier, Amsterdam, 1975.

Görgen, Hermann M., *Brazil*. Pinguin-Verlag, Innsbruck, 1981.

Guppy, Nicholas, *Tropical Deforestation: a Global View*. Foreign Affairs, Washington, 1982.

Harding, Bertita, *The Amazon Throne*. George G. Harrap, London, 1942.

Hasenbalg, Carlos A., *Race Relations in Brazil*. Latin American Institute, University of New Mexico, Albuquerque, 1985.

Hemming, John, *Red Gold*. Macmillan, London, 1978.

Henfrey, Colin, *The Gentle People*. Hutchinson, London, 1964.

Instituto Brasileiro de Análises Sociais e Economicas, *Dados da Realidade Brasileira*. Vozes, Petropolis, 1982.

Instituto Brasileiro de Análises Sociais e Economicas, *Saúde e Trabalho no Brasil*. Vozes, Petropolis, 1983.

Kent, Rockwell (introduction), *Portinari: his Life and Art*. University of Chicago Press, Chicago, 1940.

Lang, James, *Portuguese Brazil: the King's Plantation*. Academic Press, New York & London, 1979.

Latin American Bureau, *Brazil: State and Struggle*. London, 1982.

Lemos, Carlos, Roberto, José, Leite, Teixera, and Gismonti, Pedro Manuel, eds., *The Art of Brazil*. Harper & Row, New York, 1983.

Lopes, Luiz Martins, *Bulletin Mensal da Faculdade de Economia e Administração de Universidad de São Paulo*, 1984.

Marshall, Andrew, *Brazil*. Thames and Hudson, London, 1966.

Merrick, Thomas W., *Brazil's Population Since 1945*. Unpublished paper from Population Reference Bureau, Washington, 1984.

Milhaud, Darius, *Notes sans Musique*. René Julliard, Paris, 1949.

Ministerio do Industria e Commercio, Conselho de Não ferrosos e de Siderurgia, *Annuario estatistico do Brasil*, Brasilia, 1985.

Ministry of External Relations, *Brazilian Art*. São Paulo, 1976.

Nagel's Encyclopedia Guide, *Brazil*. Geneva, 1980.

Perlman, Janice E., *The Myth of Marginality*. The University of California, Berkeley, 1976.

Perry, Ritchie, *Brazil: the Land and its People*. Macdonald Educational, London, 1982.

Petroleo Brasileiro S. A. Petrobras, *Brazil: 1984*.

Phelps, Gilbert, *The Last Horizon: a Brazilian Journey*. Knight & Co., London, 1971.

Poppino, Rollie, *Brazil: the land and the people*. Oxford University Press, New York & London, 1968.

Prado, Jnr., Caio, trans. Suzette Machado, *The Colonial Background of Modern Brazil*. University of California Press, Berkeley & Los Angeles, 1967.

Rabinovitz, Francine, and Trueblood, Felicity M., eds., *Latin American Urban Research, Volume 1*. Sage, Beverley Hills, 1971.

Rivière, Paul, ed., *Peoples of the Earth, Volume 6: Amazonia, Orinoco and the Pampas*. The Danbury Press, London, 1973.

Rodrigues, José Honorio, *Brazil and Africa*. University of California Press, Berkeley, 1965.

São Paulo Justice and Peace Commission, *São Paulo—Growth and Poverty*. Bowerdean, London, 1978.

Schreider, Helen, and Schreider, Frank, *Exploring the Amazon*. National Geographic Society, Washington, 1970.

Schulthess, Emil, *The Amazon*. Simon & Schuster, New York, 1962.

Secretaria de Planejamento, *Annuario Estatistico do Brasil*. Brasília, 1983.

Singer, Paul, *Crisis of Miracle*. Paz e Terra, Rio de Janeiro, 1982.

Singer, Paul, *Dominação e Disigualdade, Estructura de Classes, e Repartição de Renda no Brasil*. Paz e Terra, Rio de Janeiro, 1981.

Skidmore, Thomas E., *Black into White*. Oxford University Press, New York, 1974.

Smith, Anthony, *Mato Grosso: Last Virgin Land*. Michael Joseph, London, 1971.

Sorjo, Bernardo, and Almeida, Tavares de, ed. Maria Herminia, *Sociedade e Politica no Brasil pos-64*. Brasiliense, São Paulo, 1983.

Sterling, Tom, *The Amazon* (The World's Wild Places Series). Time-Life International, Amsterdam, 1972.

Wagley, Charles, *An Introduction to Brazil*. Columbia University Press, New York, 1971.

Wagley, Charles, ed., *Race and Class in Rural Brazil*. Unesco, Paris, 1952.

Weil, Thomas E., *Area Handbook of Brazil*. The American University, Washington, 1975.

Wellington, Sandra I., *The Art of the Brazilian Indian*. British Museum, London, 1978.

Worth, John D., *Politics of Brazilian Development, 1930–1954*. Stanford University Press, Stanford, 1970.

Zweig, Stefan, trans. Andrew St. James, *Brazil: land of the future*. Cassell & Co., London, 1942.

PERIODICALS

Art and Artists, Special Issue Brazil, April 1976.

Bury, John, "The Little Cripple: the Genius of Brazil". *World Review*, March 1951.

Conta, Manfred von, "São Paulo: Mammon und Macumba". *Geo*, May 1979.

Financial Times Special Reports:

"The Sleeping Giant Begins to Stir", December 7, 1982.

"Poised for a New Era", November 5, 1984.

Gaede, Peter-Matthias, "Os Abandonados: die Strassenkinder von São Paulo". *Geo*, June 1985.

Georges, Eliane, "Brésil de Tous les Saints". *Geo*, May 1985.

"Itaipu: a Dam to Humble All". *Geo*, November 1981.

Kroll, Benno, "Manaus: die Erben des Untergangs". *Geo*, October 1978.

Laxalt, Robert, "Last of a Breed: the Gauchos". *National Geographic*, October 1980.

Lea, Vanessa, "Brazil's Kayapo: beset by a Golden Curse". *National Geographic*, May 1984.

Morrison, Tony, "Capital Achievement". *Telegraph Sunday Magazine*, June 16, 1985.

Rob, Gerda, "Salvador de Bahia: Stadt im Dunklen Schleier". *Geo*, May 1984.

Sa, Hernane Tavares de, "Metropolis made to Order". *National Geographic*, May 1960.

Starbird, Ethel A., "The Bonanza Bean: Coffee". *National Geographic*, March 1981.

Villas Boas, Orlando, and Villas Boas, Claudio, "Saving Brazil's Stone Age Tribes". *National Geographic*, September 1968.

INDEX

Page numbers in italics refer to illustrations or illustrated text.

A

Abaeté, Lagoa do, *39*

Abará, 124

Acuña, Father Cristóbal de, 142

Afro-Brazilian blacks: importation as slaves, 45, *47*, 48, 52, *54*; influence on cuisine, 115–116; influence on literature, 118; influence on music, 113–114, 121, 125; interbreeding with whites, 24, 45–46, *69*, 74; percentage of population, 74; present-day position, 63, 65, 73, 74, 76–77, *77*; spiritist cults, 114, 115, 117–118, *129*, *132*, *133*

Afro-Brazilian Democratic Committee, 77

Agassiz, Louis, 53

Agricultural industry: exports, 22, 97–98; failure to develop, 97–98; in Ceará, *12–13*; in Paraná, *21*; and land distribution, 98; work force, *8*, 22. *See also* Cattle; Rubber; Sugar

Aircraft manufacturing industry, 101–102

Alcohol fuel: distillation from sugar, 24, *97*, 100

Aleijadinho, O (Antônio Francisco Lisbôa), 54, 116–117; soapstone statue of Hosea, *120*

Aluminium production, 100

Amado, Jorge, 24, 33; *Dona Flor and her Two Husbands*, 121; *Gabriela, Clove and Cinnamon*, 121

Amazon, River, 21, *140–141*; discovery of, 138; first navigation of, 137; length of, 138; naming of, 137; as tourist attraction, *10*; tributaries, 138

Amazonia, 20–21, 30, 138; climate, *147*; ecological concerns for, 154–155; economic boost for, 32–33; failure of cattle ranchers in, 148, 150, 154–155; flora and fauna in, *53*, 138–139, *139*, 142, 146, *152*, *153*, 155; gold mining in, 100, 137, *143–145*, 150; Jari project, 87, 148, *149*; land speculators in, 148; mining companies in, 151; population of, 30, 32; roads in, *15*; school in, *75*; size of, 30, 138; timber reserves in, 21–22. *See also* Indians; Rubber industry; Trans-Amazonian Highway

Américo, Pedro, *51*

Andrade, Mário de: *Hallucinated City*, 120; *Macunaíma: Hero without a Character*, 121

Anteater, giant, *152*, 153

Antonil (Italian Jesuit): quoted, 46

Araguaia Indian reserve, 151

Arara Indians, 142

Araújo, Maria de, *131*

Architecture, 17, 19, 60, 123–124

Arditi, Iracema, 124–125

Aripuaña Indian reserve, 151

Armadillo, giant, *153*, 153

Arms industry, 101, 102

Army: revolts, 56–57, 60. *See* Military governments

Art: Brazilian, 123, 124–125; Indian, 121

Azevedo, Aluísio, 119

Azevedo, Fernando de: *Brazilian Culture*, 114

B

Backlands, 24–25, 33; deprivation of, 67–68, *116*, 119, 120

Bahia (state), 24; Administrative Centre exhibition palace, 124; Bom Jesus da Lapa, 117; cuisine of, *124*; independence movement in, 49; sugar industry in, 45; tobacco industry in, *88*

Bandeirantes, 16, *18*, 51

Bates, Henry Walter, 146

Bauxite mining, 22, 100

Beaches, *34–41*

Belém, 21, 139, 142

Belém-Brasília Highway, *15*, 90

Belo Horizonte, 26; Church of São Francisco, *123*; Fiat car factory, *86*

Bernades, Sérgio, 124

Birth rate, *12*, 66

Blumenau, 29

Boas, Claudio Villas, 148

Boca do Rio, *35*

Bom Jesus da Lapa, 117

Branco, Gerson Castelo, 124

Brasília: building of, 17, 19, 60, *61*, 123–124; Central Bank building, 96; inauguration date, 17, 19; parliamentary offices, *16*; population of, 19; schools in, 70

Brazil: discovery of, 43; earliest chart of, *42*; maps of, *15*, *19*; naming of, 22; topographical details of, 20–21, 28–29

Brazilian Negro Front, the, 76–77

Brazilwood tree, 22, 24, *42*, 43

British merchants, 19th-century, 49

Bureaucracy, state, 96–97

C

Cabral, Admiral Pedro Álvares, 21, 43, *54*

Caeté Indians, 45

Cameron, James: quoted, 24

Caminha, Pero Vaz de, 43

Campelo, Glanco, 124

Campos Basin, 100

Candangos, 19, 20

Candomblé (cult), 117–118, *129*

Capoeira, *126*

Capybaras, *153*

Carajás mining complex, 98, *99*, 100, 151

Cariocas, *36–37*

Carvajal, Gaspar de, 137

Casaldáliga, Dom Pedro, 154

Castro Alves, Antônio de, 118, 119

Catholic Church, 114, 116, *128*; establishes *Commissão Pastoral de Terra*, 150; and family planning, 66; and Indians, 43, 150, 154; toleration of cults by, 33, 114–115, 118, *129*; as unifying factor, 33. *See also* Jesuit missionaries

Cattle industry, *8*, 29, *78*, *79*, *82*; failure in Amazonia, 148, 150

Ceará (state), *18*; Juàzeiro do Norte, *12–13*; peasant women in, *24*

Cicero, Padre, *130*, *131*

CIMI, 154

Civil servants: corruption of, 60, 96; move to Brasília, 19, 60; salaries of, 65

Cladas, Zamine, 124

Class structure, 63–65, 66, 74, 76

Coconut palm, *34*

Coffee industry, *21*, 22, 24, 26, 28, 53, *55*, 56, 88, *91*
"Colour" groups, 22–23, 24, 33, 45–46, *69*
Commissão Pastoral de Terra (CPT), 150
Condamine, La, *see* La Condamine, Charles Marie de
Congonhas do Campo: Sanctuary of Bom Jesus, 54, 117; statue of Hosea at, *120*
Congress, Brazilian, 33, 76
Conselheiro, O (Antônio Maciel), 119–120
Construction industry, *8*, 69, 91, 93, *105*
Copacabana Beach, *6–7*, *36–37*, *40*, *41*, 52
"Copacabana 18", the, 56
Copper mining, *99*
Cordel literature, *116*
Costa, Lúcio, 17, 123–124
CPT, *see Commissão Pastoral de Terra*
Crato, *130*
Crime rates, 73, 93
Cuisine: African influence on, 115–116; in Bahia, *124*
Cults, spiritist, 114, 115; Candomblé, 117–118, *129*; Macumba, 118, *129*, *132*, *133*; of Tia Neiva, *134*, *135*
Cunha, Euclides da: *Rebellion in the Backlands*, *116*, 119–120

D
Dams: Itaipu, 55, 98, *105–111*; Tucurui, 98, *105*, 151
Darwin, Charles, 24, 146
Delfim Netto, Antônio, 90
Discrimination, *see* Racial discrimination
Divorce, 65
Domestic servants, 65, 67
Dutch settlers, 43; expulsion of, 54
Dutra, General Eurico Gaspar, 59

E
Economy, 87–102
Educational system: schools, 70, *75*; universities, 64
Electoral system, 33
Embraer aircraft company, 101–102
Estado Novo (New State), 58–59
Estancias (ranches), *78*

F
Family, extended: importance of, 63, 64–65
Farming, *see* Agricultural industry
Favelas (shanty towns), 20, 28, *67*, 71–2, 74
FEBEM depots, 73
Feminist movement, 65–67
Fernandes, Millor, 76
Fiat car factory, Belo Horizonte, *86*, 102
Figueiredo, President, 66
Fleming, Peter: quoted, 26
Football, *41*, *112*, 126
Ford, Henry, 146–147
Ford Motor Company, *86*, 90, 102
France: French colonists, 43, 44–45; French influence, 49
Freyre, Gilberto: *The Masters and the Slaves*, 63, 76, 116
FUNAI (National Indian Foundation), 148, 151
Fur trade, *30*

G
Gama, Vasco da, 43
Gaúchos, *8–9*, 29, *78–85*
Geisel, General Ernesto, 66, 92
General Motors, *86*, 90, 102
Gil, Gilberto, 126
Goiás (state), 30, 47; Araguaia Indian reserve, 151
Gold mining and prospectors, 22, 24, 25, *16–18*, 100; on Serra Pelada, *143–145*, 150
Gondwanaland, 138
Gorotire Indian reserve, 151, 154
Goulart, João, 60, 90
Gouvea, Andrés de: quoted, 45
Government: democratic, 60, 96–97, 98, 100; military, 53, 59–60, 90–94, 96, 97–98
Grasslands, *8*, 29, 78
Guanabara Bay, 44–45, 49
Guedalla, Philip: quoted, 28

H
Hammocks, *127*, 142
Horto, *20*
Humboldt, Friedrich von, 146

I
Iguaçu Falls *27*, 30
IMF, *see* International Monetary Fund
Immigrants, 29, 49, 56, 64, *72*, 74; Czech, 64; German, 29, *73*; Italian, 64; Japanese, 56, 64, *72*, 74
Inconfidência Mineira, 26, *48–49*
Independence movements, 26, 48–49
Indians: Amazonian, 142, 146, 147, 148, 151, *154*; art and crafts, 121, 142; conversion to Christianity, 43, *44*, 45, 115, 116; and early settlers, 43, 45, 142; hostility to pioneers, 46, *48*; influence on Villa-Lobos, 121, 122; Kadiweu, 121; Kayapo, 151, 154; Kuikuru, 121; medicinal knowledge of, 155; National Indian Foundation (FUNAI), 148, 151; Parakana, 151; parks and reserves, 151, 154; and racial prejudice, 23; romanticization of, 120–121; Service for the Protection of Indians, 147, 151; Tapirapé, 142; Tucano, 121; Tupinambá, 45; Txukarramrae, *154*; Yanomamo, 142, 154
International Monetary Fund, 93, 96
Ipiranga, Cry of, 51, *51*
Iron ore deposits, 22, 26, *99*, 100
Isabel, Princess Regent, 52
Itaipu Dam, 55, 98, *105–111*

J
Jaguars, *30*, *153*
Jari river, *147*; Jari project, 87, 148, *149*
Jefferson, Thomas, 48
Jesuit missionaries, 44, *44*, 45, 54, 115, 142, 146
João III, King of Portugal, 44
João, Dom (later João VI, King of Portugal), 49, 54–55
João Pessoa: Hotel Tambaú, 124
Juàzeiro do Norte, *12–13*, *131*

K
Kadiweu Indians, 121
Kayapo Indians, 151, 154
Kubitschek, Juscelino, 55, 59–60, 89–90; and building of Brasília, 17, 60
Kuikuru Indians, 121

L
Lacerda, Carlos, 59
La Condamine, Charles Marie de, 146
Lampião ("The Lantern"), *58*, *59*
Language, 29, 33, 114
Le Corbusier (Charles-Édouard Jeanneret), 123
Lisbôa, Antônio Francisco, *see* Aleijadinho, 0
Literature, *116*, 118–121
Ludwig, Daniel K., 87, 148
Lula (Luiz Inácio da Silva), 94

M
Machado de Assis, Joaquim Maria, 118–119
Maciel, Antônio, *see* Conselheiro, 0
Macumba (cult), 118, *129*, *132*, *133*
Madeira, River, *127*, 150
Madrid, Treaty of, 54
Maloca, *154*
Manaus: as centre of rubber industry, 53, 56; as duty-free port, 32, *100*; homes and offices by S. M. Porto in, 124; Opera House at, 53, 55, *94*, *95*; waterfront at, *56*
Manganese deposits, 22, *99*
Manufacturing industries, *8*, 88, 102
Maria, Queen of Portugal, 49
Mato Grosso (state), *15*, 30, 47; Indian reserves in, 151; new towns in, *137*
Milhaud, Darius, 125–126
Military governments, 53, 59–60; and the economy, 53, 90–94, 96, 97–98
Minas Gerais: churches in, 116; joins Liberal Alliance, 56; Minas Conspiracy, 26, 48–49; mining in, 25–26, 46, 47
Mining industry, *8*, 22, 98, *99*, 100; in 17th and 18th centuries, 25–26, 46. *See also* Gold mining
Miranda, Carmen, 119
Modernist movement, 120
Mortality rate, infant, *12*, 30, 71
Mota Silva, Djanira da, 124
Motor industry, 24, 68, *86*, 88, 90, 91, *96*, 102
Mulatos, 74, 76
Music and musicians, 55, 113–114, *118*, 121–123, 125–126

N
Napoleon Bonaparte, 49
Nascimento, Abdias do, 77
Negro, River, *56*, 138; Tucano Indians, 121
Neiva, Tia, *134*
Nepotism, 64–65
Neves, Tancredo, 96
Newspapers, 63, 76
Niemeyer, Oscar, 17, 19, 60, *123*, 124
Northern Perimeter Highway, *15*
Novacap, 17, 19
Nuclear power programme, 92, 97, 100

O

Oil industry, 22, 89, *96*, 100
Olinda: Carnival in, 113
Orellana, Francisco de, 137
Otter, giant, *152, 153*
Ouro Prêto, 25–26, *28*; churches, 116

P

Pampas, *8*, 29, 78
Pan-American Highway, *15*
Pará (state), *15*, 146–147; Beiradão, *147*; Tumucumaque Indian Park, 151
Paraguai, River, 121
Paraguay, River, 21
Parakana Indians, 151
Paraná (state), *21*, 29; coffee plantations in, *91*
Paraná, River, 21, 29. *See also* Itaipu Dam
Parentela, 63, 64–65
Peçanha, President Nilo, 76
Pedro I, Dom, 49, 51, *51*
Pedro II, Dom, 51–53
Pernambuco, 68; independence movement in, 49; sugar plantations in, 45
Petrobras, 89, 96, 100
Piauí: house by G. C. Branco at, 124
Pinzón, Captain Vincente Yáñez, 138
Piranha, *53*
Plastic surgery industry, 67
Political system, 33, 53
Population, *12*; "colour" groups, 23; distribution, *19*, 23; growth, 22
Portinari, Cândido, 123; *Café, 122*; mural of St. Francis, *123*
Porto, Severiano Mario, 124
Pôrto Velho, *15*
Portuguese: colonists, 22, 43–44, 45; emigration of, 48; take over direct rule of Brazil, 49, 51
Poverty, 67–68, 71–73
Prado, Paulo: *Portrait of Brazil*, 121
PT (Workers' Party), 94, 96

Q

Qaratem, Nunzio, 101
Quadros, Jânio, 60, 90
Quinine, discovery of, 146

R

Racial discrimination, 23, 76–77, *77*; Unified Black Movement against Racial Discrimination, 77
Railways, 51–52, 89, 92, 97
Recife, 21; early settlements around, 24
Religion, *see* Catholic Church; Cults, spiritist
Republic, establishment of the, 52–53
Rio de Janeiro, *6–7*, 26, 28; arrival of British merchants in, 49; beaches at, 21, 26, *34*; Botanical Gardens, 49; capital transferred to, 48; Carnival in, *10–11*, 28, 113, *114*; crime in, 73; establishment of, 44–45; *favelas* in, 28, *67*; first hotel in, 49; gold as foundation of wealth in, 25, 26; independence movement in, 49; Macumba shrine, *133*; National Development Bank building, 96; National Housing Bank building, 96; Petrobras building, 96; under

Prince Regent Dom João, 49; Sambódromo, *10*; Urca, *70*
Rio Grande do Norte: Areia Branca salt pans, *92*
Rio Grande do Sul, 29; *gaúchos* in, *8–9*; joins Liberal Alliance, 56
Road construction, *15, 30*, 32–33, 89, 90, 91, 97, 98, 148
Rolim de Moura, 150
Rondon, Cândido Mariano da Silva, 147
Rondônia (state), *15*, 147, 150, *150*
Roosevelt, Eleanor, 27
Roosevelt, Theodore, *53*, 146
Roraima (state): Yanomamo reserve, 154
Rubber industry, 24, 32, 53, 56, 88, 146–147
Rubinstein, Artur, 122–123

S

Salaries: civil servants', 65; doctors', 65
Salvador, *103*; beaches in, 21, *34, 35, 39*; as capital, 24, 26, 44, 48; Carnival in, *114*; Church of Our Lord of Bonfim (Nosso Senhor do Bonfim), 117–118, *129*; Convento do Carmo, *128*; *favela* houses in, *67*; street stalls in, *124*
Samba, the, 113–114, 125, 126; *Pelo Telefone*, 55, 113; schools for learning, *10–11*, 113
Santa Catarina (state), *73*
Santos, 21
São Bernardo, 68, 69, 90; Metalworkers' Union, 94
São Francisco river, 21
São Luís, 119
São Paulo, *23*, 28; anti-fascism demonstration in (1978), 77; *bandeirantes* in, 46; car factories in, 68, 69; coffee oligarchy in, 56; crime rate in, 73, 93; *favelas* in, 71, 93; foundation of, 44; gold as foundation of wealth in, 25; homeless children in, *64*, 72–73; Japanese quarter, *72*; migration to, 28, 68–69; population of, *23*, 28; rebellion in (1932), 57; suburbs of, 90; Week of Modern Art (1922), *55*, 120
São Vicente, 44, 45
Sarney, President José, 96, 98
Sassi, Mario, *134*
Schlesinger, Arthur: quoted, 19
Schools, 70, *75*
Schultes, Richard, 155
Sculpture, 115, 116–117, *120*, 124
Serra Pelada: gold mine, *143–145*, 150
Sertão, the, *see* Backlands
Servants, domestic, 65, 67
Service for the Protection of Indians (SPI), 147, 151
Silva, Luiz Inácio da, *see* Lula
Slave trade, *see* Afro-Brazilian blacks
Sloths: arboreal, *153*; three-toed, *152*
Sousa, Admiral Martim Alfonso de, 43–44
Sousa, Governor General Tomé de, 44
Soya production, 97
SPI, *see* Service for the Protection of Indians
Spiritist cults, *see* Cults, spiritist
Spix, J. B. de, *53*
Steel industry, 59, 88, 89, 92, 102
SUDAM, 96, 148
SUDECO, 96

SUDENE, 96
SUDESUL, 96
Suffrage, female, 57
Sugar industry, *13, 20*, 24, 25, 45, 46, 88; and distillation of alcohol, *97*, 100

T

Tapirapé Indians, 142
Tenentes, 56, 57
Timber industry, 21–22, 24, *32*, 87
Tiradentes, see Xavier, J. J. da Silva
Tobacco industry, 22, 46, *88*
Tomlinson, H. M.: quoted, 30
Tordesillas, Treaty of, 54
Trade unions, 57, 89, 90, 94
Trans-Amazonian Highway, *15, 30*, 32–33, 91, 97, 98, 148
Tucano Indians, 121
Tucurui Dam, 98, *105*, 151
Tumucumaque Indian Park, 151
Tupinambá Indians, 45
Txukarramrae Indians, 154

U

Unemployment, 93
Universities, 64
Uranium deposits, 100, 154
Uruguay, River, 21, 29

V

Valley of the Dawn, *134*
Vaqueiros, 24
Vargas, Getúlio, *55*, 56–59, 77, 88, 89
Vatapá, 124
Vieira, Father António, *44*, 146
Villa-Lobos, Heitor, 55, *118*, 121–123
Volkswagen motor company, *86*, 90, 102
Volta Redonda steel mills, 59, 89

W

Wallace, Alfred Russel, 146
Water resources, *105*
White Arrow, *134*
Wickham, Henry, 56
Wildlife, *53*, 138–139, 146, *152, 153*
Women, *see* Feminist movement
Wood pulp industry, 87, 148, *149*
Workers' Party (PT), 94, 96
World War I, 56
World War II, 29, 58–59, 65

X

Xavier, Joaquim José da Silva (*Tiradentes*), 26, 48–49
Xingu Indian reserve, 151
Xingu river: Kuikuru Indians, 121; Txukarramrae Indians, 154

Y

Yanomamo Indians, 142, 154
Yemanjá (African god), *132, 133*

Z

Zweig, Stefan, 120

Colour separations by Fotolitomec, S.N.C., Milan, Italy. Typesetting by Tradespools Ltd., Somerset, England. Printed and bound by Artes Gráficas, Toledo, S.A., Spain.